Algebra Survival Guide

Workbook

by Josh Rappaport,
author of the
Algebra Survival Guide

Algebra Survival Guide Workbook

Thousands of Problems to Sharpen Skills
and Enhance Understanding

Published by:
Singing Turtle Press
942 Vuelta del Sur
Santa Fe, NM 87507

Tel: 1/505-438-3418
Mobile: 1/505-690-2351
Fax: 1/512-682-0500
www.SingingTurtle.com
E-mail: info@SingingTurtle.com

First printing 2003. Additional printings: 2004, 2005, 2006, 2007, 2008, 2009, 2010, 2012, 2013

ISBN-10: 0-9659113-7-3

ISBN-13: 978-0-9659113-7-5

SINGING
TURTLE
P R E S S

The publisher expresses heartfelt appreciation to Paul Obrecht for his superb technical consulting and mathematical typesetting services.
A big thanks, too, to David Cox for his digital background photos, all shot in Santa Fe, New Mexico.
Thanks — as always — to Sally Blakemore, for her inspired artwork, ongoing support, and joyful marimba music.
Last but not least, thanks to the author's family, for patience and inspiration.

— Attention Teachers / Administrators —
For information on volume discounts to schools, visit us at: SingingTurtle.com
Or call us at the phone number above.

Contents

Welcome to the Workbook!

Flipping through this Workbook, you can see it's packed with thousands of practice problems ... and answers to every single one of them (not just to the odds!). But for whom is this Workbook intended, and how does one make optimal use of it?

This book is for **EVERYONE** who wants help **LEARNING** or **TEACHING PRE-ALGEBRA** and **ALGEBRA 1**. That means it's for **TEACHERS, TUTORS, PARENTS, STUDENTS, HOMESCHOOLERS,** precocious young **MATH WHIZZES, ADULTS** returning to school ... leaving anyone out? Let me know.

How does one use the Workbook? It's best used along with my *Algebra Survival Guide* **(ASG)**, also published by Singing Turtle Press. That's because the Workbook's problem sets are keyed to the pages of the *Algebra Survival Guide*. If you have the Guide, you know that it provides clear instructions on how to do every problem set in this Workbook, along with conversational explanations of the concepts. If you don't have the Guide, get a copy now to reap the greatest benefit from this Workbook.

Here are some special ways the Workbook can help you!

➤ Each problem set focuses on just **ONE SPECIFIC SKILL**. I've found that children are most likely to succeed at algebra if they first learn a skill, then master it through **PLENTY OF PRACTICE**. This Workbook gives them that chance to understand and excel.

➤ Many problem sets use not only numbers and variables, but also **SYMBOLS** and **FUNNY WORDS**. The symbols and funny words are not just for entertainment. When children see symbols and words in algebraic rules and formulas, it gives them a way to **GRASP THE FORMULA IN ITS MOST GENERAL SENSE**. This helps them retain the concepts, for they understand them more deeply.

➤ Like the Guide, the Workbook teaches children not only **WHAT TO DO**, but also **WHAT <u>NOT</u> TO DO**. Learning the **PITFALLS TO AVOID** is as important as learning the correct algebraic procedures.

➤ The Workbook serves as a springboard for **FUN AND CREATIVE PROJECTS**. Example: Once children master a problem set, encourage them to make up a set of problems just like the ones they now understand. Then have them exchange problems with other children, or with their parents. Come up with your own extensions.

I'm confident that this Workbook will enhance your ability to teach or learn algebra. Best of luck on your ongoing trek through the Algebra Wilderness!

— Josh Rappaport

Which properties, if any, are shown by these statements — reflexive, symmetric, or transitive?

See ASG, pp. 9–11

1) $ab = ab$ _____
2) If $6x = 12$, then $x = 2$ _____
3) If $6x = 12$, then $12 = 6x$ _____
4) If $a = r$, and $r = q$, then $a = q$ _____
5) If $a = b$, and $g = h$, then $a = h$ _____
6) If $5b = a$, then $a = 5b$ _____
7) If $2x = y$, and $y = 4z$, then $2x = 4z$ _____
8) $m = n = p$ _____
9) If $m = m$, and $n = n$, then $m = n$ _____
10) If $5 \cdot 2 = 10$, then $10 = 5 \cdot 2$ _____

_____ %

Which properties, if any, are shown by these statements — associative, commutative, or distributive?

See ASG, pp. 12–15

1) $4(3 + 2) = 4 \cdot 3 + 4 \cdot 2$ _____
2) $4 \cdot (3 \cdot 2) = (4 \cdot 3) \cdot 2$ _____
3) $6 + 2 = 2 + 6$ _____
4) $7(x + y) = 7x + 7y$ _____
5) $m \cdot n = n \cdot m$ _____
6) $16 \div 2 = 2 \div 16$ _____
7) $x(y + z) = xy + xz$ _____
8) $x(y + z) = (x \cdot y) + z$ _____
9) $x \cdot (y \cdot z) = (x \cdot y) \cdot z$ _____
10) $12 + (a + b) = (12 + a) + b$ _____

_____ %

Which properties, if any, are shown by these statements — additive identity or multiplicative identity?

See ASG, pp. 17–18

1) $5 \cdot 1 = 5$ _____
2) $m + 0 = m$ _____
3) $7x \cdot 1 = 7x$ _____
4) $r \cdot 0 = r$ _____
5) $42c + 0 = 42c$ _____
6) $(a \cdot b) \cdot 0 = (a \cdot b)$ _____
7) $a + 1 = a$ _____
8) $a \cdot 1 = 1$ _____
9) $(4a + 3b) \cdot 1 = 4a + 3b$ _____
10) $(3m + 5n) + 0 = 3m + 5n$ _____

_____ %

To which sets of numbers, if any, do the following belong — natural (N), whole (W), or integer (I)?

See ASG, pp. 23–25

1) 4 _____
2) – 1 _____
3) 7 _____
4) 0 _____
5) – 12 _____
6) 14/3 _____
7) – 123 _____
8) 147 _____
9) 3.2 _____
10) 6/11 _____

11) 18,482 _____
12) 1 _____
13) – 8.5 _____
14) – 87 _____
15) 63.7 _____
16) 81 _____
17) – 81 _____
18) 6,351 _____
19) – 785 _____
20) – 10/3 _____

_____ %

To which sets of numbers, if any, do the following belong — rational (R) or irrational (I)?

See ASG, pp. 26–28

1) 82 _____
2) $\sqrt{5}$ _____
3) 7.63582196... _____
4) 1.125 _____
5) $\sqrt{13}$ _____
6) 4.12701270... _____
7) 2/9 _____
8) $\sqrt{2}$ _____
9) 61 _____
10) 4.444... _____
11) 43.121212... _____
12) 1.1024697... _____
13) 480/713 _____
14) 1/4 _____
15) π _____
16) 8.063258196... _____
17) 8.06325 _____
18) 14.0691436... _____
19) 1.111... _____
20) $\sqrt{24}$ _____

_____ %

Simplify using the same-sign rule.

See ASG, pp. 36–38

1) + 2 + 1 _____
2) + 4 + 3 _____
3) – 6 – 4 _____
4) + 1 + 7 _____
5) – 8 – 4 _____
6) – 1 – 2 _____
7) + 7 + 6 _____
8) + 6 + 9 _____
9) – 7 – 3 _____
10) – 6 – 5 _____
11) + 11 + 8 _____
12) – 14 – 7 _____
13) – 9 – 12 _____
14) + 7 + 18 _____
15) + 15 + 2 _____

16) – 16 – 9 _____
17) + 21 + 21 _____
18) – 21 – 18 _____
19) – 15 – 15 _____
20) + 17 + 17 _____
21) + 6 + 3 + 5 _____
22) + 8 + 4 + 2 _____
23) – 6 – 3 – 7 _____
24) + 10 + 8 + 6 _____
25) – 11 – 7 – 8 _____
26) – 14 – 1 – 5 _____
27) + 1 + 4 + 13 _____
28) + 3 + 16 + 8 _____
29) + 15 + 15 + 15 _____
30) – 8 – 16 – 32 _____

31) + 1 + 2 + 3 + 4 _____
32) – 2 – 4 – 6 – 8 _____
33) – 3 – 6 – 9 – 12 _____
34) + 4 + 8 + 12 + 16 _____
35) + 2 + 10 + 4 + 12 _____
36) – 6 – 7 – 8 – 9 _____
37) – 4 – 12 – 1 – 6 _____
38) + 13 + 8 + 4 + 1 _____
39) + 18 + 21 + 6 + 13 _____
40) – 8 – 7 – 1 – 17 _____
41) + 1 + 3 + 5 + 7 + 9 _____
42) + 2 + 6 + 5 + 1 + 4 _____
43) + 2 + 2 + 2 + 2 + 2 _____
44) – 8 – 3 – 1 – 4 – 9 _____
45) – 14 – 6 – 5 – 5 – 10 _____
46) + 2 + 4 + 4 + 5 + 6 _____
47) + 12 + 6 + 4 + 6 + 4 + 8 _____
48) – 13 – 7 – 6 – 8 – 12 _____
49) + 15 + 16 + 10 + 9 + 12 + 4 _____
50) – 11 – 17 – 5 – 18 – 6 – 22 _____

_____%

Simplify using the mixed-sign rule.　　See ASG, pp. 39–41

1) + 2 – 1 _____	36) – 42 + 52 _____
2) + 4 – 3 _____	37) + 63 – 23 _____
3) – 5 + 2 _____	38) – 72 + 36 _____
4) – 4 + 6 _____	39) + 19 – 47 _____
5) + 8 – 2 _____	40) + 86 – 41 _____
6) – 4 + 2 _____	41) + 26 – 18 _____
7) + 5 – 3 _____	42) – 12 + 43 _____
8) – 7 + 8 _____	43) – 17 + 16 _____
9) + 7 – 3 _____	44) + 29 – 14 _____
10) + 4 – 2 _____	45) – 16 + 31 _____
11) – 8 + 3 _____	46) + 62 – 41 _____
12) + 7 – 6 _____	47) + 17 – 62 _____
13) + 7 – 5 _____	48) + 43 – 39 _____
14) – 9 + 6 _____	49) – 86 + 62 _____
15) + 6 – 9 _____	50) + 97 – 72 _____
16) – 8 + 2 _____	51) + 100 – 200 _____
17) – 2 + 7 _____	52) – 151 + 153 _____
18) – 3 + 9 _____	53) + 182 – 150 _____
19) + 9 – 1 _____	54) – 260 + 180 _____
20) + 9 – 8 _____	55) + 476 – 273 _____
21) – 11 + 8 _____	56) + 815 – 453 _____
22) + 3 – 35 _____	57) + 750 – 250 _____
23) + 6 – 22 _____	58) – 681 + 412 _____
24) + 4 – 14 _____	59) + 999 – 633 _____
25) + 48 – 8 _____	60) + 873 – 384 _____
26) – 4 + 17 _____	61) + 331 – 368 _____
27) – 7 + 13 _____	62) – 823 + 134 _____
28) + 6 – 15 _____	63) + 198 – 473 _____
29) + 15 – 6 _____	64) + 183 – 496 _____
30) – 27 + 9 _____	65) – 552 + 914 _____
31) + 18 – 28 _____	66) + 959 – 267 _____
32) – 16 + 23 _____	67) – 657 + 833 _____
33) – 21 + 34 _____	68) – 551 + 951 _____
34) + 15 – 45 _____	69) – 265 + 374 _____
35) – 18 + 32 _____	70) + 597 – 899 _____

_____ %

First write S or M to show if you use the same-sign rule (S) or the mixed-sign rule (M). Then simplify.

See ASG, pp. 36–40

	Problem	S or M	Simplify
1)	– 3 – 7		
2)	+ 3 – 7		
3)	+ 3 + 7		
4)	– 3 + 7		
5)	– 8 + 5		
6)	+ 8 – 5		
7)	– 8 – 5		
8)	+ 8 + 5		
9)	– 6 + 2		
10)	+ 9 + 4		
11)	+ 13 – 6		
12)	+ 13 + 8		
13)	– 1 + 14		
14)	– 8 – 12		
15)	+ 4 + 17		
16)	+ 15 + 30		
17)	+ 13 – 23		
18)	– 10 + 18		
19)	– 21 + 18		
20)	+ 17 – 13		

_____ %

Simplify using the same- or mixed-sign rule.

See ASG, p. 42

1) + 4 – 3 + 2 _____
2) + 5 – 4 + 3 _____
3) – 6 – 4 + 5 _____
4) – 7 + 15 – 8 _____
5) + 8 + 4 – 10 _____
6) + 18 – 6 + 3 _____
7) + 11 – 22 – 33 _____
8) + 17 + 13 – 14 _____
9) – 26 – 13 + 19 _____
10) + 4 – 18 – 8 + 6 _____

11) + 4 + 18 + 8 + 6 _____
12) – 4 + 18 + 8 – 6 _____
13) – 21 – 14 – 55 + 10 _____
14) + 46 – 17 – 13 + 14 _____
15) + 81 – 25 – 36 + 10 _____
16) + 8 – 102 + 42 + 11 _____
17) – 273 + 61 – 9 + 186 _____
18) + 636 – 363 – 131 – 11 _____
19) + 512 – 256 + 128 + 64 _____
20) – 225 – 121 + 49 + 9 _____

_____ %

When solving equations, you often encounter the same- or mixed-sign rule in a vertical format. So expressions like + 3 + 5 or – 4 + 7 will appear as

$$\begin{array}{r} + 3 \\ + 5 \\ \hline \end{array} \quad \text{or} \quad \begin{array}{r} - 4 \\ + 7 \\ \hline \end{array}$$

NEW CONCEPT!

Don't let this vertical format throw you. Here's a chance to practice.

Combine the following terms using the same-sign rule.

_____ %

1) + 4
    + 6

2) – 17
    – 4

3) + 18
    + 9

4) – 43
    – 17

5) – 8
    – 37

Combine the following terms using the mixed-sign rule.

_____ %

1) + 2
    – 7

2) – 12
    + 18

3) + 62
    – 45

4) – 48
    + 39

5) – 27
    + 55

Combine the following terms using either the same- or mixed-sign rule.

1) + 13
    + 24

2) – 18
    + 21

3) + 25
    – 21

4) – 16
    – 15

5) – 25
    + 36

6) – 21
    + 35

7) + 24
    + 28

8) + 18
    – 27

9) + 21
    + 35

10) – 13
    – 41

11) – 37
    + 57

12) – 11
    – 45

13) + 17
    – 62

14) + 42
    – 18

15) – 13
    – 36

16) + 21
    + 52

17) + 45
    + 31

18) – 52
    – 39

19) – 23
    + 47

20) + 28
    – 35

21) – 46
    + 51

22) + 45
    + 28

23) – 23
    – 56

24) + 32
    – 55

25) + 62
    + 89

26) – 58
    – 36

27) – 41
    + 68

28) + 87
    – 53

29) + 85
    + 37

30) – 91
    + 66

_____ %

10

First show what happens after using the neighbor-sign rule. Then write S or M to show if you use the same- or mixed-sign rule. Then simplify.

See ASG, pp. 43–47

Problem	After using neighbor-sign rule	S or M	Simplify
1) − 3 + (− 2)			
2) − 8 + + 5			
3) + 7 − − 4			
4) − 9 − (+ 7)			
5) + 6 + − 7			
6) + 8 + + 4			
7) − 7 − − 3			
8) + 2 − + 2			
9) − 1 − (− 8)			
10) − 4 + − 6			
11) + 12 + (+ 8)			
12) − 7 + − 17			
13) + 24 − + 9			
14) + 4 − − 31			
15) − 46 + − 8			
16) + 27 − (+ 35)			
17) − 61 − − 45			
18) − 86 + − 52			
19) − 76 + + 63			
20) + 21 − (− 81)			
21) − 126 + − 804			
22) + 312 − + 392			
23) + 181 − (− 406)			
24) − 240 + − 376			
25) + 621 + + 412			

_____ %

Simplify. See ASG, p. 48

1) $-6 + (-8) + 3$ _____

2) $+1 - 1 + -7$ _____

3) $-4 - -2 + 4 + -3$ _____

4) $-5 + 4 - -1$ _____

5) $+9 - 8 + (-5)$ _____

6) $-8 - +6 + 9 - -1$ _____

7) $+7 - 2 - -6$ _____

8) $+7 + (-5) + 5$ _____

9) $+4 + (+1) - (+3) - 4$ _____

10) $-6 + 8 + -5 - +1$ _____

11) $-3 + -12 + -5 + +17$ _____

12) $+21 - -1 - +43 + -8 + -8$ _____

13) $-9 - +24 - -4 - +52$ _____

14) $-86 - (-7) + (+41) - (-1) - (+62)$ _____

15) $+5 + 18 + -9 + +61$ _____

16) $-38 - +9 - +80 - -2 + -4$ _____

17) $+46 - -61 - -2 + -14 - -82$ _____

18) $+54 - (+72) + (-86) - (+6) + (-16)$ _____

19) $+5 + +63 - +42 + -28 - +81$ _____

20) $-84 - -3 + -91 + +30 + -52$ _____

_____ %

Simplify using the multiplication rule. See ASG, pp. 49–50

1) $(+3) \cdot (-2)$ _____ 6) $(-8) \cdot (+3) \cdot (-2)$ _____

2) $(-6) \cdot (+4)$ _____ 7) $(-8) \cdot (-14) \cdot (-4)$ _____

3) $(+8) \cdot (+7)$ _____ 8) $(-18) \cdot (+3) \cdot (-9)$ _____

4) $(+4) \cdot (-13)$ _____ 9) $(-6) \cdot (+10) \cdot (+5)$ _____

5) $(-16) \cdot (-4)$ _____ 10) $(+4) \cdot (-1) \cdot (-17)$ _____

_____ %

Simplify using the division rule.   See ASG, p. 51

1) $(+24)/(-3)$ _____
2) $(+18)/(+6)$ _____
3) $(-16)/(+4)$ _____
4) $(-20)/(-6)$ _____
5) $(+35)/(+7)$ _____

6) $(-46)/(-2)$ _____
7) $(+19)/(-4)$ _____
8) $(+63)/(+9)$ _____
9) $(+80)/(-10)$ _____
10) $(-99)/(+11)$ _____

_____ %

Tell which operation comes before which other one, then simplify.   See ASG, p. 59

1) $(25 - 16)^2$ _____
2) $(8 + 1) \cdot (4 \div 2)$ _____
3) $2^2 - 4^2$ _____
4) $(2 - 4)^2$ _____
5) $3^2 \cdot 4^2$ _____
6) $+ 3 - 4 - 9 + 2$ _____
7) $16/4 + 6$ _____
8) $(4 + 3) - (8 + 1)$ _____
9) $(8 \cdot 2) - 6^2$ _____
10) $2^2 + 6^2$ _____

_____ %

Don't simplify. Just tell which enclosure marks you'd work out first, second, and possibly third in the following problems.   See ASG, p. 60

1) $[(3 + 6) \div 5] \cdot 2$ _____
2) $\{3 + (4 + 6)^2\}$ _____
3) $([8 - \{4 + 6\}^2 \div 12] - 8)^2$ _____
4) $[8 + \{(26 - 8) \div 4\}] \div 2$ _____
5) $|(4 - 3)^2 - 86|$ _____
6) $16 + (8 + 3 \cdot [4 - 8]) \div 2$ _____
7) $|([16 - 32] \cdot 16) - 100|$ _____
8) $\{(|8 - 16| \cdot 8) - 50\} + 2$ _____
9) $[4 \cdot 3\{8 + |2 - 4|\} \div 62] + 4$ _____
10) $\{[(8 + 7)^2 - 100] \div 5\} + 20$ _____

_____ %

Use the order of operations to simplify the following problems. See ASG, p. 62

1) $4^2 + 8(3 \cdot 2)$ _____

2) $3 + [8 - (4 + 3)^2]$ _____

3) $2(4 + 3) + (-16)(4 - 6)$ _____

4) $\{15 - (3 \cdot 2)\} \div 3$ _____

5) $3^2 - (-1) + (-30 \div 2)$ _____

6) $7 + ([3 - 7] + 4^2) \div 2$ _____

7) $(-6) - (4 \cdot 3)(3 - 1) - 2^2$ _____

8) $(3 + 4)^2$ _____

9) $(3^2 + 4^2)$ _____

10) $5 - [(4 \cdot 5) \div 2]$ _____

11) $\{[(3 + 5) \div 2]^2 - (3 \cdot 2)\} \cdot (-2)$ _____

12) $[(4 \cdot 6) - (3 \cdot 2)] \div 2$ _____

13) $[3^2 - (2^2 \cdot 4)] + 7$ _____

14) $3 + \{(4 + 3) \cdot 6 - 2\}$ _____

15) $\{(8 - 3) \cdot 4 - [6(2 + 3) - 10]\} + 4$ _____

16) $(2)(3) + (3)(4) - (4)(5)$ _____

17) $[8 + (4)(5)] \div (2 - 6)$ _____

18) $(40 \cdot 2) \div [(12 \cdot 2) - 4]$ _____

19) $7 \cdot 8 \div 4 - 20$ _____

20) $15 \cdot 3 \div 5 + 12 \div 2$ _____

_____ %

Multiply and divide. See ASG, p. 63

1) $50 \div 5 \times 2$ _____

2) $50 \times 2 \div 5$ _____

3) $50 \div 5 \div 2$ _____

4) $50 \div (5 \times 2)$ _____

5) $50 \div 2 \times 5$ _____

6) $50 \times 5 \div 2$ _____

7) $50 \times (5 \div 2)$ _____

8) $6 \times 3 \div 2$ _____

9) $3 \div 2 \times 6$ _____

10) $2 \div 3 \times 6$ _____

11) $3 \times 2 \div 6$ _____

12) $4 \times 7 \div 2 \times 3$ _____

13) $4 \times 7 \times 3 \div 2$ _____

14) $3 \div 2 \times 4 \times 7$ _____

15) $4 \times 3 \div 2 \div 6$ _____

16) $4 \div 3 \times 2 \times 6$ _____

17) $4 \times 3 \div (2 \times 6)$ _____

18) $4 \div 2 \times 3 \div 6$ _____

19) $2 \times 3 \div 4 \times 6$ _____

20) $2 \times 3 \div (4 \times 6)$ _____

_____ %

14

Simplify.

See ASG, p. 64

1)	$2 \cdot 3^2$	_____	1a)	$(2 \cdot 3)^2$	_____
2)	$4 \cdot 2^2$	_____	2a)	$(4 \cdot 2)^2$	_____
3)	$2 \cdot 4^2$	_____	3a)	$(2 \cdot 4)^2$	_____
4)	$4 \cdot 3^2$	_____	4a)	$(4 \cdot 3)^2$	_____
5)	$3 \cdot 4^2$	_____	5a)	$(3 \cdot 4)^2$	_____
6)	$(2 \cdot 6)^2$	_____	6a)	$2 \cdot 6^2$	_____
7)	$(5 \cdot 3)^2$	_____	7a)	$5 \cdot 3^2$	_____
8)	$7 \cdot 2^2$	_____	8a)	$(7 \cdot 2)^2$	_____
9)	$2 \cdot 7^2$	_____	9a)	$(2 \cdot 7)^2$	_____
10)	$(5 \cdot 2)^2$	_____	10a)	$5 \cdot 2^2$	_____

_____ %

Simplify.

See ASG, p. 65

1)	-2^2	_____	1a)	$(-2)^2$	_____
2)	-3^2	_____	2a)	$(-3)^2$	_____
3)	-4^2	_____	3a)	$(-4)^2$	_____
4)	-5^2	_____	4a)	$(-5)^2$	_____
5)	-6^2	_____	5a)	$(-6)^2$	_____
6)	$(-7)^2$	_____	6a)	-7^2	_____
7)	$(-8)^2$	_____	7a)	-8^2	_____
8)	-9^2	_____	8a)	$(-9)^2$	_____
9)	$(-10)^2$	_____	9a)	-10^2	_____
10)	-11^2	_____	10a)	$(-11)^2$	_____

_____ %

Tell whether or not these terms are like terms.

See ASG, p. 67

1)	6, 3/5, $-7/12$	_____	6) $3a^2b$, a^2b, $4ba^2$	_____
2)	mn, 3mp, 2np	_____	7) $2mcq$, mq^2c, $2qmc$	_____
3)	xyz, yzx, zxq	_____	8) $a^2x^2m^2$, $4m^2a^2x^2$, $\frac{1}{4}m^2x^2a^2$	_____
4)	1/4, 0.363, $-4/3$	_____	9) $0.25rq$, qr, $\frac{1}{5}rq$	_____
5)	df^2e, $4def^2$, $2dfe^2$	_____	10) ah^2m, m^2ha, a^2hm	_____

_____ %

Add or subtract like terms.

See ASG, p. 68

1) $3m + 2m$ _____

2) $2q - q$ _____

3) $4rmx - 3rmx$ _____

4) $ab + ab + ab$ _____

5) $c^2d + c^2d$ _____

6) $2rm - mr$ _____

7) $z^2 + z^2$ _____

8) $5t^2v - 3vt^2$ _____

9) $3aq - aq - 2aq$ _____

10) $4x^2z + zx^2$ _____

_____ %

Make up funny names for like terms.

See ASG, p. 70

Example:

$8b - 3b$ *think:* _8 bananas – 3 bananas = 5 bananas_

So: _8b – 3b = 5b_

1) $4a + 2a$ *think:* _____

So: _____

2) $3x + 2x$ *think:* _____

So: _____

3) $6m - 2m$ *think:* _____

So: _____

4) $4r + r$ *think:* _____

So: _____

5) $5c - 2c$ *think:* _____

So: _____

6) $4y + y + y$ *think:* _____

So: _____

7) $2b - 2b$ *think:* _____

So: _____

8) $6f - 3f - 2f$ *think:* _____

So: _____

9) $2r^2 + 3r^2$ *think:* _____

So: _____

10) $4mn - 2mn$ *think:* _____

So: _____

_____ %

When solving equations, expressions that combine like terms often appear in a vertical format. For example, expressions like + 2x + 7x or − 3b + 8b can appear as:

$$\begin{array}{c} + 2x \\ + 7x \\ \hline \end{array} \quad \text{or} \quad \begin{array}{c} - 3b \\ + 8b \\ \hline \end{array}$$

NEW CONCEPT!

Just use the same- or mixed-sign rule. Here are some practice problems.

Combine the following terms using the same-sign rule.

1) + 3x	2) − 14y	3) + 8m	4) − 19a	5) − 13q
+ 7x	− 5y	+ 18m	− 3a	− 15q

_____ %

Combine the following terms using the mixed-sign rule.

1) + 4n	2) − 16p	3) + 13c	4) − 11d	5) + 15r
− 9n	+ 7p	− 18c	+ 24d	− 22r

_____ %

Combine the following terms using either the same- or mixed-sign rule.

1) + 11f	2) + 4x	3) − 15c	4) − 16h	5) + 18e
+ 8f	− 19x	+ 11c	− 12h	− 23e

6) + 17d	7) + 8w	8) − 21x	9) + 10v	10) − 9b
− 12d	+ 13w	+ 13x	+ 7v	− 18b

11) + 16d	12) − 22a	13) − 13z	14) − 11m	15) − 8r
− 25d	− 15a	+ 28z	+ 18m	− 24r

16) + 23u	17) + 6t	18) − 13q	19) + 4c	20) − 16m
+ 18u	+ 17t	− 18q	− 19c	+ 18m

21) + 13b	22) + 26s	23) − 18p	24) − 14k	25) + 21h
− 24b	+ 19s	− 19p	+ 23k	+ 25h

26) − 23n	27) + 19a	28) − 11j	29) + 25g	30) + 18y
− 17n	− 28a	+ 27j	+ 17g	− 25y

_____ %

Simplify.

See ASG, p. 71

1) $mn + 2mn$ _____

2) $4mq - 7mq$ _____

3) $- 6rx - 2rx$ _____

4) $- 3bcx + 2bcx$ _____

5) $rx^2 + rx^2$ _____

6) $- dq^2 - 2dq^2$ _____

7) $3mp + - mp$ _____

8) $n^2c - + n^2c$ _____

9) $- fv + 3fv$ _____

10) $- gh - 2hg$ _____

11) $4pt + + 2pt$ _____

12) $3r^2nw - 2r^2nw$ _____

13) $xq - 5qx$ _____

14) $b^2c + b^2c + b^2c$ _____

15) $def - 3fed$ _____

16) $- 3r^2nz + 5r^2nz$ _____

17) $abc + 3abc + - 4abc$ _____

18) $p^2 + 3.2p^2 - 1.1p^2$ _____

19) $- 12r^2pq - + 16pqr^2$ _____

20) $- 3bdf^2 - - 5df^2b$ _____

_____ %

Simplify.

See ASG, p. 72

1) $x + y + 2x + y$ _____

2) $m - 1 - m + 3$ _____

3) $2q - 3q + 3 + 1$ _____

4) $5bc + - 2df - - 3df + bc$ _____

5) $- 6xz + 6 - + 4 + 5xz$ _____

6) $hn - 2hn + bq - 2bq$ _____

7) $m - 4m + 2 + 3.2$ _____

8) $- y^2 + y + 3y^2 - 3y$ _____

9) $2cd^2 - 3f - - f + 6d^2c$ _____

10) $6xy + 5/6 - + 2xy + - 3/6$ _____

11) $6np - 4pr - 3pn + 2rp$ _____

12) $3n^2 + 4 - - 3 + - 3n^2 - 7$ _____

13) $8qh - + qt - 2qh - + 2qt$ _____

14) $5p^2 + 6p - 3p^2 - 2p^2$ _____

15) $ty - 2.25 + + 3ty - 1.75$ _____

16) $r^2 + pr + 3r^2 - + 3pr$ _____

17) $2n^2x + 3xn^2 + - 3 - - 7.3$ _____

18) $5xy - 2xy + yz - - 2yz + xy$ _____

19) $- 3r^2 + mt + - 3mt + - 4r^2$ _____

20) $2r^2qb - + rqb + 3bqr + 3qbr^2$ _____

_____ %

Simplify.   See ASG, p. 73

1) + (a + b) _____   11) + (−3 + x) _____
2) + (a − b) _____   12) − (n + p + 2) _____
3) − (a + b) _____   13) + (p + r − 3) _____
4) − (a − b) _____   14) − (a − b − c) _____
5) − (y + 6) _____   15) − (−2 + q) _____
6) + (y − 6) _____   16) + (m − n + p) _____
7) + (y + 6) _____   17) − (d + e − 6) _____
8) − (y − 6) _____   18) − (−x − y − z) _____
9) − (3 + g) _____   19) + (p − q − r) _____
10) − (6 − m) _____   20) − (−a − 4 + c) _____

_____ %

Simplify.   See ASG, p. 74

1) 8 + (a − 3) _____
2) 4 − (b + 3) _____
3) 6 − (3 − c) _____
4) 5 + (d − 2) _____
5) 2 + (e − 5) _____
6) 3 − (f + 3) _____
7) − 7 + (3 − g) _____
8) 4 − (6 + h) _____
9) 5 + (j − 6) _____
10) − 8 − (10 − k) _____
11) 2 + (−m − 2) _____
12) 7 − (−n − 8) _____
13) 7 + (p + 8) _____
14) − 3 − (q − 6) _____
15) − 5 + (r − 5) _____
16) 2 − (5 + s) _____
17) 6 + (t − 6) _____
18) − 9 + (−6 − u) _____
19) 7 − (v + 3) _____
20) − 1 − (w − 1) _____

_____ %

Determine the value.

See ASG, p. 78

1) $|4|$ _____

2) $|-4|$ _____

3) $|-2/3|$ _____

4) $|42|$ _____

5) $|-1.6|$ _____

6) $|7.25|$ _____

7) $|-7.25|$ _____

8) $|-5/6|$ _____

9) $|5/6|$ _____

10) $|-9|$ _____

_____%

Simplify.

See ASG, p. 79

1) $|1 + 3 - 6|$ _____

2) $|4 \cdot 5|$ _____

3) $|(-4)(5)|$ _____

4) $|3(2 - 6)|$ _____

5) $|36/6|$ _____

6) $|-36/6|$ _____

7) $|3 - (4 \cdot 3) + 7|$ _____

8) $|5 + (2 \cdot 3) - 11|$ _____

9) $|(3)(-2) - 6|$ _____

10) $|(-3)(4) - (3)(4)|$ _____

_____%

Simplify.

See ASG, p. 80

1) $2 + |3 - 8|$ _____

2) $6 - |4 + 3|$ _____

3) $2 \cdot |2 - 4|$ _____

4) $|(3)(-2)| - 3$ _____

5) $|(3)(-2) - 6| - 15$ _____

6) $|3 \cdot 4| \div 2$ _____

7) $|(3)(-4)| \div 2$ _____

8) $|(3)(-4)| \div (-2)$ _____

9) $|(2)(-5) - 5| - 5$ _____

10) $10 \div |7 + (3)(-4)|$ _____

11) $(-15) \div |3 \cdot 2 - 1|$ _____

12) $-4 - |(-9)(2) \div 3|$ _____

13) $8 + |(3)(-6) + 14|$ _____

14) $|8 - (3)(4)| - 4$ _____

15) $3 + |(5)(-2) + 1| - 16$ _____

_____%

Simplify. See ASG, p. 81

1) $(-3) \cdot |3 - 5|$ _____
2) $|3 - 9|/2$ _____
3) $|6 - 2|^2$ _____
4) $-10/|6 - 11|$ _____
5) $(-5) \cdot |5 - 6|$ _____
6) $(-2) \cdot |3 - 8|^2$ _____
7) $|12 - 3|/3$ _____
8) $|8 - 2| \cdot |4 - 8|$ _____
9) $|4 - 8|^2 - 17$ _____
10) $|6 - 3|^2$ _____
11) $5 \cdot |7 - 9|$ _____
12) $-3 - |2 \cdot 5|$ _____
13) $|(-2)(6)|^2$ _____
14) $100/|(-5)(5)|$ _____
15) $(|-7| \cdot |4|)/(-2)$ _____
16) $12 \cdot |12 - 15|$ _____
17) $|14 - 6 \cdot 3| \cdot (-4)$ _____
18) $|-5|^2/5$ _____
19) $3^3/|4^2 - 5^2|$ _____
20) $|7 - 12| \cdot (7 - 12)$ _____

_____ %

Simplify. See ASG, p. 82

1) $+ |-5|$ _____
2) $- |+8|$ _____
3) $- |-9|$ _____
4) $+ |+7|$ _____
5) $+ |-9|$ _____
6) $9 - |-2|$ _____
7) $- 8 + |-6|$ _____
8) $6 - |+5|$ _____
9) $5 - |-3|$ _____
10) $3 - |+5|$ _____

_____ %

Work out the values of the following exponential terms.   See ASG, p. 86

1) 3^2 _____
2) n^2 _____
3) n^3 _____
4) 2^3 _____
5) $(4x)^2$ _____

6) 3^3 _____
7) b^3 _____
8) 8^2 _____
9) $(pq)^2$ _____
10) $(1/4)^2$ _____

_____ %

Simplify. (Write each answer as a term to a power.)   See ASG, p. 89

1) $3^8 \cdot 3^2$ _____
2) $w^2 \cdot w^6$ _____
3) $4^m \cdot 4^n$ _____
4) $6^2 \cdot 6^4$ _____
5) $aardvark^2 \cdot aardvark^5$ _____
6) $p^3 \cdot p^6$ _____
7) $4^3 \cdot 4^8$ _____
8) $2^{hip} \cdot 2^{hop}$ _____
9) $r^2 \cdot r^{10}$ _____
10) $6^x \cdot 6^y$ _____

11) $10^4 \cdot 10^{10} \cdot 10^6$ _____
12) $a^6 \cdot a^9$ _____
13) $\triangle^9 \cdot \triangle^6$ _____
14) $c^8 \cdot c^7$ _____
15) $12^2 \cdot 12^8$ _____
16) $t^{2n} \cdot t^{3n}$ _____
17) $a^b \cdot a^c$ _____
18) $\diamond^3 \cdot \diamond^6$ _____
19) $87^{16} \cdot 87^{20}$ _____
20) $(xy)^w \cdot (xy)^z$ _____

_____ %

Simplify.   See ASG, p. 91

1) $\dfrac{3^{10}}{3^6}$ _____

2) $\dfrac{w^{10}}{w^6}$ _____

3) $\dfrac{5^6}{5^2}$ _____

4) $\dfrac{\bullet^9}{\bullet^4}$ _____

5) $\dfrac{8^a}{8^b}$ _____

6) $\dfrac{a^{10}}{a^2}$ _____

7) $\dfrac{tic^{tac}}{tic^{toe}}$ _____

8) $\dfrac{(p+q)^r}{(p+q)^s}$ _____

9) $\dfrac{\heartsuit^{12}}{\heartsuit^5}$ _____

10) $\dfrac{m^d}{m^d}$ _____

_____ %

When solving a problem like $(3x) \cdot (5x^2)$, first multiply the coefficients together, then multiply the variables together. Then string the two answers together. So to simplify $(3x) \cdot (5x^2)$, first multiply $3 \cdot 5 = 15$. Then multiply $x \cdot x^2 = x^3$. String the two answers together to get $15x^3$ as the final answer.

NEW CONCEPT!

1) $4y \cdot 2y$ _____

2) $6p^2 \cdot 7p$ _____

3) $2m^2 \cdot 3m^2$ _____

4) $5b^4 \cdot 5b^3$ _____

5) $4x^2 \cdot 8x^3$ _____

6) $12v \cdot v$ _____

7) $6t \cdot 2t^8$ _____

8) $3a^4 \cdot 4a^6$ _____

9) $9f \cdot 6$ _____

10) $10c^3 \cdot 5c^3$ _____

11) $5 \cdot 8w$ _____

12) $3e^2 \cdot 5e^2$ _____

13) $y \cdot 4y$ _____

14) $2p \cdot 3p \cdot 4p^2$ _____

15) $2x \cdot 3x^2 \cdot 5x^3$ _____

_____ %

When solving a problem like $12a^5/4a^3$, first divide the coefficients, then divide the variable terms, then put the two together. In this example, first divide 12 by 4 to get 3. Then divide a^5 by a^3 to get a^2. Put the two answers together to get the final answer, $3a^2$.

NEW CONCEPT!

1) $\dfrac{6m^2}{3m}$ _____

2) $\dfrac{9r^3}{3r}$ _____

3) $\dfrac{12p^4}{3p}$ _____

4) $\dfrac{15q^5}{3q}$ _____

5) $\dfrac{15m^{12}}{5m^4}$ _____

6) $\dfrac{10a}{5a}$ _____

7) $\dfrac{12e^3}{12e}$ _____

8) $\dfrac{7y}{7}$ _____

9) $\dfrac{3t^8}{2t^4}$ _____

10) $\dfrac{7x}{7x}$ _____

11) $\dfrac{18p^x}{3p^y}$ _____

12) $\dfrac{21d^{10}}{3d^2}$ _____

13) $\dfrac{6c^7}{3c^2}$ _____

14) $\dfrac{4x^{11}}{2x^5}$ _____

15) $\dfrac{8d^5}{2d^2}$ _____

_____ %

Simplify the following expressions.   See ASG, pp. 88 and 94

1) 3^1 _____
2) 3^0 _____
3) $(-10)^0$ _____
4) $(-10)^1$ _____
5) π^0 _____

6) π^1 _____
7) 7.865^0 _____
8) 12^1 _____
9) 162^1 _____
10) $(-14/3)^0$ _____

_____ %

Simplify the following expressions.   See ASG, p. 95

1) a^4b^0 _____
2) $6 - 4^0$ _____
3) $10 + w^0$ _____
4) $x^2y^4z^0$ _____
5) $x^0 + y^0 + a$ _____
6) mn^2p^0 _____

7) $m \cdot n^2 \cdot 4p^0$ _____
8) $r^2 - t^0$ _____
9) $\dfrac{a^3b^2c}{xy^0z^4}$ _____
10) $\dfrac{6 - a^0}{8 + a^0}$ _____

_____ %

Arrange the terms in descending order.   See ASG, p. 97

1) $-3 + y$ _____
2) $2y + y^2 - 6$ _____
3) $-m + 3 - m^2$ _____
4) $3b^2 + 2b^3 - 4 - 3b$ _____
5) $13 + n^2$ _____
6) $-c + 3 + 2c^2$ _____
7) $p^2 - 3p^3 + 9 - 2p^4 + 6p$ _____
8) $-3x + x^5 + 7$ _____
9) $9a - 5 + a^3 - 2a^2$ _____
10) $3e^2 - 2e + 5$ _____
11) $r^2 - 3r^3 + 4 - r + 8r^4$ _____
12) $2t^2 + 5 - t + 12t^3$ _____
13) $-5q - 3q^2 + 5$ _____
14) $3w^4 - 4w^3 + 6 - 2w^2 + 8w^5 - w$ _____
15) $5 + s - s^2 - s^3$ _____

_____ %

Rewrite the following terms using only positive exponents.   See ASG, p. 98

1) x^{-2} _____

2) b^{-4} _____

3) c^{-8} _____

4) $\diamond^{-5}$ _____

5) 9^{-2} _____

6) 7^{-n} _____

7) $12^{-earring}$ _____

8) y^{-x} _____

9) cat^{-dog} _____

10) 8^{-m} _____

_____ %

Rewrite the following terms using only positive exponents.   See ASG, p. 100

1) $\dfrac{1}{2^{-7}}$ _____

2) $\dfrac{1}{p^{-6}}$ _____

3) $\dfrac{1}{3^{-x}}$ _____

4) $\dfrac{1}{\oplus^{-w}}$ _____

5) $\dfrac{1}{ski^{-snowboard}}$ _____

6) $\dfrac{1}{r^{-6}}$ _____

7) $\dfrac{1}{8^{-c}}$ _____

8) $\dfrac{1}{pizza^{-slice}}$ _____

9) $\dfrac{1}{\diamondsuit^{-3}}$ _____

10) $\dfrac{1}{7^{-1}}$ _____

_____ %

Rewrite the following terms using only positive exponents.   See ASG, p. 102

1) $3x^{-2}y^{-3}$ _____

2) $x^{3}y^{-2}$ _____

3) $\dfrac{2m^{2}n^{-4}}{5p^{4}r^{-3}}$ _____

4) $\dfrac{7}{a^{-2}b^{-3}c^{-5}}$ _____

5) $\dfrac{d^{-2}}{e^{-3}}$ _____

6) $r^{2}f^{-3}x^{-5}j^{8}$ _____

7) $6p^{2}r^{-2}$ _____

8) $\dfrac{n^{2}x^{3}p^{-4}}{6^{-2}m^{2}r^{-2}}$ _____

9) $\dfrac{3^{-2}xy^{2}}{5^{-2}m^{3}n^{-2}}$ _____

10) $\dfrac{a^{-n}b^{-m}c^{-p}}{d^{-x}e^{-y}f^{-z}}$ _____

_____ %

Simplify, keeping all exponents positive. See ASG, p. 103

1) $\dfrac{2^7}{2^3}$ _____

2) $\dfrac{x^{12}}{x^5}$ _____

3) $\dfrac{4^2}{4^5}$ _____

4) $\dfrac{clone^6}{clone^{11}}$ _____

5) $\dfrac{m^3}{m^{-5}}$ _____

6) $\dfrac{z^{15}}{z^2}$ _____

7) $\dfrac{10^{-6}}{10^2}$ _____

8) $\dfrac{lemur^{-8}}{lemur^{-11}}$ _____

9) $\dfrac{r^{-2}}{r^{-1}}$ _____

10) $\dfrac{n^6}{n^{13}}$ _____

_____ %

Simplify, keeping all exponents positive. See ASG, p. 104

1) $\dfrac{r^2 r^{-2}}{r^3 r^4 r^2}$ _____

2) $\dfrac{m^{-3} m^4}{m^{-6} m^2}$ _____

3) $\dfrac{3^{-2} \cdot 3^{-3} \cdot 3^{-4}}{3^4 \cdot 3^5 \cdot 3^6}$ _____

4) $\dfrac{x^{-6} x^2}{x^{-8} x^3}$ _____

5) $\dfrac{eel^{-4} \cdot eel^2}{eel^{-11} \cdot eel^{-4}}$ _____

6) $\dfrac{c^3 c^8}{c^{-5} c^{-4}}$ _____

7) $\dfrac{z^{-2} z^{-4} z^{-1}}{z^{-3} z^{-5} z^6}$ _____

8) $\dfrac{pony^{-8} \cdot pony^3}{pony^{12} \cdot pony^{-6}}$ _____

9) $\dfrac{6^{10} \cdot 6^{-17} \cdot 6^4}{6^{-6} \cdot 6^{-2}}$ _____

10) $\dfrac{v^{-3} v^2}{v^{11} v^{-13} v^2}$ _____

_____ %

Simplify, keeping all exponents positive. See ASG, p. 105

1) $\dfrac{a^2 b^{-4}}{b^{-3} a^{-4}}$ _____

2) $\dfrac{3^{-3} r^4}{r^{-2} 3^{-2}}$ _____

3) $\dfrac{4^{-4} w^6}{w^2 w^{-4} 4^{-5}}$ _____

4) $\dfrac{t^5 v^{-3} v^4}{v^{-5} t^7}$ _____

5) $\dfrac{8^{12} n^{-3} 8^{-4}}{n^4 8^{10}}$ _____

6) $\dfrac{c^8 e^5 e^{-3}}{c^6 e^2 c^2}$ _____

7) $\dfrac{d^{-7} 5^{-3}}{5^2 d^{-5} d^{-9} 5^{-8}}$ _____

8) $\dfrac{9^{-5} z^2 z^{-8} 9^{12}}{z^5 9^9}$ _____

9) $\dfrac{k^{17} u^{12} u^{-4}}{k^9 k^{13} u^2}$ _____

10) $\dfrac{s^{15} 7^{-13} 7^0 s^{-18}}{7^6 7^{-20} s^{-3}}$ _____

_____ %

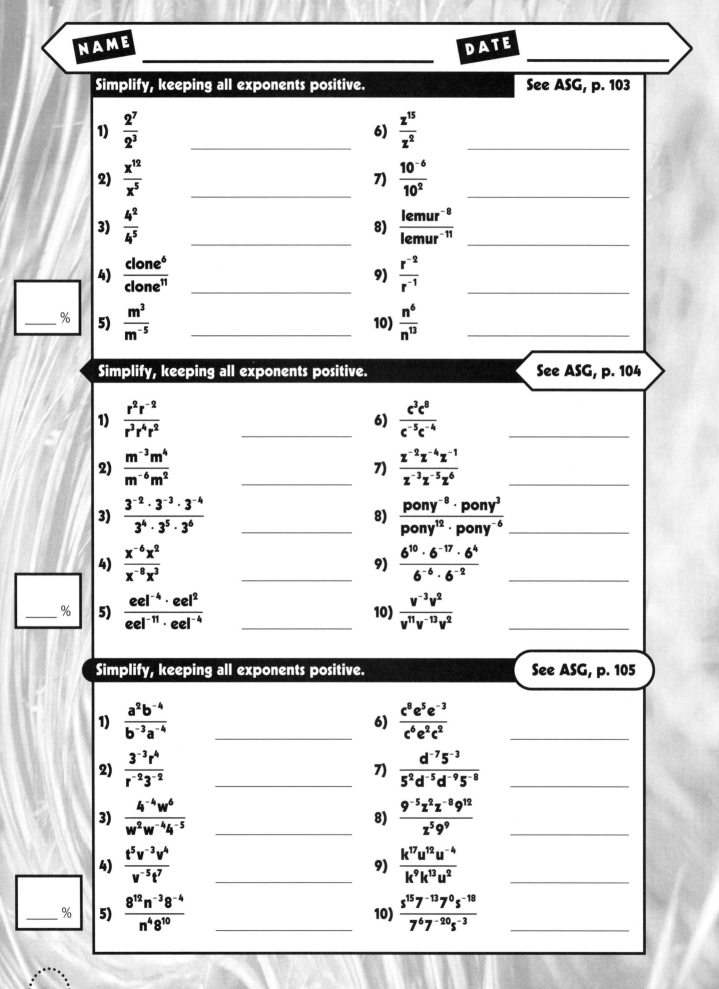

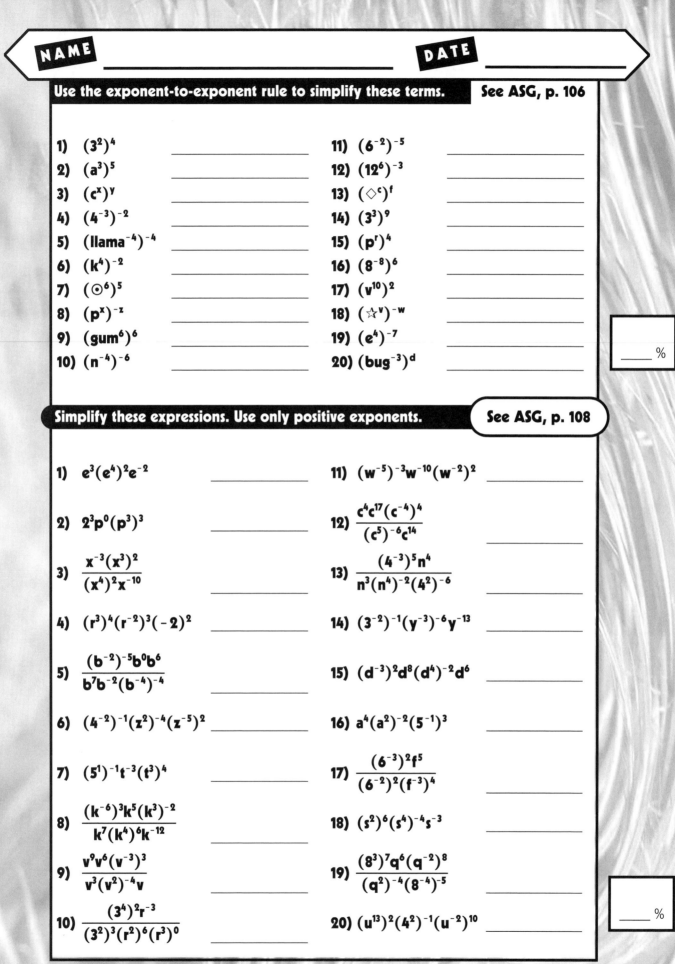

Use the exponent-to-exponent rule to simplify these terms.   See ASG, p. 106

1) $(3^2)^4$ _____

2) $(a^3)^5$ _____

3) $(c^x)^y$ _____

4) $(4^{-3})^{-2}$ _____

5) $(llama^{-4})^{-4}$ _____

6) $(k^4)^{-2}$ _____

7) $(\odot^6)^5$ _____

8) $(p^x)^{-z}$ _____

9) $(gum^6)^6$ _____

10) $(n^{-4})^{-6}$ _____

11) $(6^{-2})^{-5}$ _____

12) $(12^6)^{-3}$ _____

13) $(\diamond^c)^f$ _____

14) $(3^3)^9$ _____

15) $(p^r)^4$ _____

16) $(8^{-8})^6$ _____

17) $(v^{10})^2$ _____

18) $(\star^v)^{-w}$ _____

19) $(e^4)^{-7}$ _____

20) $(bug^{-3})^d$ _____

_____ %

Simplify these expressions. Use only positive exponents.   See ASG, p. 108

1) $e^3(e^4)^2e^{-2}$ _____

2) $2^3p^0(p^3)^3$ _____

3) $\dfrac{x^{-3}(x^3)^2}{(x^4)^2x^{-10}}$ _____

4) $(r^3)^4(r^{-2})^3(-2)^2$ _____

5) $\dfrac{(b^{-2})^{-5}b^0b^6}{b^7b^{-2}(b^{-4})^{-4}}$ _____

6) $(4^{-2})^{-1}(z^2)^{-4}(z^{-5})^2$ _____

7) $(5^1)^{-1}t^{-3}(t^3)^4$ _____

8) $\dfrac{(k^{-6})^3k^5(k^3)^{-2}}{k^7(k^4)^6k^{-12}}$ _____

9) $\dfrac{v^9v^6(v^{-3})^3}{v^3(v^2)^{-4}v}$ _____

10) $\dfrac{(3^4)^2r^{-3}}{(3^2)^3(r^2)^6(r^3)^0}$ _____

11) $(w^{-5})^{-3}w^{-10}(w^{-2})^2$ _____

12) $\dfrac{c^4c^{17}(c^{-4})^4}{(c^5)^{-6}c^{14}}$ _____

13) $\dfrac{(4^{-3})^5n^4}{n^3(n^4)^{-2}(4^2)^{-6}}$ _____

14) $(3^{-2})^{-1}(y^{-3})^{-6}y^{-13}$ _____

15) $(d^{-3})^2d^8(d^4)^{-2}d^6$ _____

16) $a^4(a^2)^{-2}(5^{-1})^3$ _____

17) $\dfrac{(6^{-3})^2f^5}{(6^{-2})^2(f^{-3})^4}$ _____

18) $(s^2)^6(s^4)^{-4}s^{-3}$ _____

19) $\dfrac{(8^3)^7q^6(q^{-2})^8}{(q^2)^{-4}(8^{-4})^{-5}}$ _____

20) $(u^{13})^2(4^2)^{-1}(u^{-2})^{10}$ _____

_____ %

Simplify. Just use the product-to-exponent rule.   See ASG, p. 109

_____%

1) $(3 \cdot 5)^2$ _____
2) $(x \cdot y)^4$ _____
3) $(4 \cdot 7)^{-p}$ _____
4) $(a \cdot b)^x$ _____
5) $(tooth \cdot eye)^4$ _____

6) $(6 \cdot 3)^{-d}$ _____
7) $(2 \cdot 4 \cdot 5)^3$ _____
8) $(\triangle \cdot \square)^z$ _____
9) $(p \cdot q)^{-2}$ _____
10) $(c \cdot e)^y$ _____

To simplify a term like $(3x)^2$, first apply the exponent to the coefficient, 3, to get 3^2 or 9. Then apply the exponent to the variable to get x^2. Then string the answers together to get $9x^2$.

NEW CONCEPT!

1) $(5y)^2$ _____
2) $(2z)^3$ _____
3) $(-3a)^2$ _____
4) $(4b)^3$ _____
5) $(3n)^2$ _____
6) $(-2d)^3$ _____
7) $(6c)^2$ _____
8) $(4h)^2$ _____
9) $(5e)^3$ _____
10) $(-7f)^2$ _____
11) $(8g)^2$ _____
12) $(-2b)^3$ _____
13) $(6p)^3$ _____
14) $(2r)^3$ _____
15) $(-4t)^2$ _____

16) $(3a)^4$ _____
17) $(7k)^2$ _____
18) $(-6m)^3$ _____
19) $(2z)^4$ _____
20) $(4j)^3$ _____
21) $(3w)^3$ _____
22) $(-6x)^2$ _____
23) $(7y)^3$ _____
24) $(4p)^4$ _____
25) $(-9n)^3$ _____
26) $(3q)^3$ _____
27) $(-4u)^3$ _____
28) $(-8s)^3$ _____
29) $(2v)^3$ _____
30) $(10x)^3$ _____

_____%

Simplify, keeping all exponents positive.
See ASG, p. 110

1) $a^2(ba)^{-2}b$ _____

2) $7^{-2}e^{-3}(ce)^4$ _____

3) $\dfrac{w^2v(wv)^{-2}}{v^{-3}w^5(vw)^2}$ _____

4) $(pq)^3p^{-2}(pq)^{-2}q^4$ _____

5) $\dfrac{3^{-2}(rn)^4r^{-6}}{r^{-2}(3^{-1})n^{-2}}$ _____

6) $\dfrac{(3z)^{-2}z^8t}{t^3(3z^2)^{-4}z^6}$ _____

7) $9^{-2}y^{15}(xy)^{-3}(x^2y^2)^{-4}$ _____

8) $k^{-3}(yk)^4k^{-2}y^8$ _____

9) $\dfrac{a^2(ac)^5c^2}{c^{-2}(ac)^{-2}}$ _____

10) $(6m)^3d^2m^0(6m^2)^{-1}m^4$ _____

_____ %

Simplify these terms using the quotient-to-exponent rule.
See ASG, p. 111

1) $\left(\dfrac{m}{n}\right)^6$ _____

2) $\left(\dfrac{2}{5}\right)^3$ _____

3) $\left(\dfrac{\triangle}{\square}\right)^x$ _____

4) $\left(\dfrac{t}{w}\right)^c$ _____

5) $\left(\dfrac{3}{7}\right)^{-2}$ _____

6) $\left(\dfrac{2}{9}\right)^3$ _____

7) $\left(\dfrac{x}{y}\right)^{-3}$ _____

8) $\left(\dfrac{r}{c}\right)^{-p}$ _____

9) $\left(\dfrac{\bigstar}{\square}\right)^{\triangle}$ _____

10) $\left(\dfrac{3}{10}\right)^{-4}$ _____

_____ %

Simplify, keeping all exponents positive.
See ASG, p. 112

1) $\left(\dfrac{r}{m}\right)^4 \cdot \dfrac{m^2}{r^3}$ _____

2) $\dfrac{c^2b^{-3}}{b^2c^3} \cdot \left(\dfrac{b}{c}\right)^4$ _____

3) $\dfrac{3^2t^2}{3^4w^2} \cdot \left(\dfrac{t}{w}\right)^5$ _____

4) $\left(\dfrac{a}{c}\right)^{-3} \cdot \left(\dfrac{a}{c}\right)^5$ _____

5) $\dfrac{r^2}{e^{-6}} \cdot \left(\dfrac{2^2e^2}{2^3r^{-2}}\right)^{-1}$ _____

6) $\left(\dfrac{v}{n}\right)^{-3} \cdot \left(\dfrac{n}{v}\right)^{-6}$ _____

7) $\left(\dfrac{5^2}{5^3}\right)^{-3} \cdot \dfrac{dr^2}{d^3r}$ _____

8) $\dfrac{b^2}{c^5} \cdot \left(\dfrac{c}{b}\right)^{-3}$ _____

9) $\left(\dfrac{7^3}{7^4}\right) \cdot \dfrac{m^2n^{-3}}{n^{-5}m^{-6}}$ _____

10) $\left(\dfrac{2}{5}\right)^{-2} \cdot \dfrac{2^3 \cdot 5^2}{2^4 \cdot 5^6}$ _____

_____ %

Find the square roots.

See ASG, p. 116

1) $\sqrt{16}$ _____   6) $\sqrt{100}$ _____

2) $\sqrt{25}$ _____   7) $\sqrt{81}$ _____

3) $\sqrt{4}$ _____   8) $\sqrt{169}$ _____

4) $\sqrt{64}$ _____   9) $\sqrt{121}$ _____

5) $\sqrt{49}$ _____   10) $\sqrt{196}$ _____

_____ %

Find the value.

See ASG, p. 119

1) $\sqrt{25} \cdot \sqrt{25}$ _____   6) $\sqrt{c} \cdot \sqrt{c}$ _____

2) $\sqrt{12a} \cdot \sqrt{12a}$ _____   7) $\sqrt{19} \cdot \sqrt{19}$ _____

3) $\sqrt{7mn^2} \cdot \sqrt{7mn^2}$ _____   8) $\sqrt{36xy} \cdot \sqrt{36xy}$ _____

4) $\sqrt{w} \cdot \sqrt{w}$ _____   9) $\sqrt{salami} \cdot \sqrt{salami}$ _____

5) $\sqrt{\dfrac{1}{4}} \cdot \sqrt{\dfrac{1}{4}}$ _____   10) $\sqrt{16p^2q^2} \cdot \sqrt{16p^2q^2}$ _____

_____ %

Find the value.

See ASG, p. 120

1) $(\sqrt{18})^2$ _____   6) $(\sqrt{q})^2$ _____

2) $(\sqrt{m})^2$ _____   7) $(\sqrt{8w^2})^2$ _____

3) $(\sqrt{rt})^2$ _____   8) $(\sqrt{mnp})^2$ _____

4) $(\sqrt{1/8})^2$ _____   9) $(\sqrt{100x^2y})^2$ _____

5) $(\sqrt{☺})^2$ _____   10) $(\sqrt{magic})^2$ _____

_____ %

Find the perfect squares of the following terms.

See ASG, p. 123

1) 13 _____   6) 1/5 _____

2) y _____   7) 12p _____

3) 31 _____   8) 18 _____

4) 15 _____   9) 111 _____

5) r^2 _____   10) 10xy _____

_____ %

Combine the radicals.

See ASG, pp. 124–125

1) $3\sqrt{8} - + 5\sqrt{8}$ _____

2) $2\sqrt{7} - 8\sqrt{7}$ _____

3) $\sqrt{4} + 9\sqrt{4}$ _____

4) $6\sqrt{2} - - 7\sqrt{2}$ _____

5) $-4\sqrt{12} - 9\sqrt{12}$ _____

6) $-11\sqrt{u} + + 2\sqrt{u}$ _____

7) $15\sqrt{v} - 6\sqrt{v}$ _____

8) $-15\sqrt{a} - 6\sqrt{a}$ _____

9) $-13\sqrt{t} + - 3\sqrt{t}$ _____

10) $9\sqrt{x} + 8\sqrt{x}$ _____

_____ %

Combine using the radical product rule.

See ASG, p. 126

1) $\sqrt{2} \cdot \sqrt{5}$ _____

2) $\sqrt{3} \cdot \sqrt{7}$ _____

3) $\sqrt{a} \cdot \sqrt{c}$ _____

4) $\sqrt{d} \cdot \sqrt{x}$ _____

5) $\sqrt{6} \cdot \sqrt{y}$ _____

6) $\sqrt{a} \cdot \sqrt{13}$ _____

7) $\sqrt{frog} \cdot \sqrt{toad}$ _____

8) $\sqrt{rain} \cdot \sqrt{cloud}$ _____

9) $\sqrt{☆} \cdot \sqrt{□}$ _____

10) $\sqrt{△} \cdot \sqrt{☺}$ _____

_____ %

Use the radical product rule.

See ASG, p. 127

1) $\sqrt{3} \cdot \sqrt{12}$ _____

2) $\sqrt{2} \cdot \sqrt{8}$ _____

3) $\sqrt{16} \cdot \sqrt{4}$ _____

4) $\sqrt{6} \cdot \sqrt{24}$ _____

5) $\sqrt{18} \cdot \sqrt{8}$ _____

6) $\sqrt{7} \cdot \sqrt{28}$ _____

7) $\sqrt{a} \cdot \sqrt{a}$ _____

8) $\sqrt{m} \cdot \sqrt{m}$ _____

9) $\sqrt{3x} \cdot \sqrt{27x}$ _____

10) $\sqrt{4y} \cdot \sqrt{49y}$ _____

11) $\sqrt{9x} \cdot \sqrt{x}$ _____

12) $\sqrt{25c} \cdot \sqrt{4c}$ _____

13) $\sqrt{11e} \cdot \sqrt{11e}$ _____

14) $\sqrt{2k} \cdot \sqrt{18k}$ _____

15) $\sqrt{72p} \cdot \sqrt{2p}$ _____

16) $\sqrt{7w} \cdot \sqrt{7w}$ _____

17) $\sqrt{3z} \cdot \sqrt{3z} \cdot \sqrt{9}$ _____

18) $\sqrt{2} \cdot \sqrt{5u} \cdot \sqrt{10u}$ _____

19) $\sqrt{2} \cdot \sqrt{4n} \cdot \sqrt{8n}$ _____

20) $\sqrt{2r} \cdot \sqrt{7r} \cdot \sqrt{14}$ _____

_____ %

Split the squares.

See ASG, p. 128

1) $\sqrt{8 \cdot 5}$ _____

2) $\sqrt{11 \cdot 7}$ _____

3) $\sqrt{m \cdot p}$ _____

4) $\sqrt{x \cdot y}$ _____

5) $\sqrt{15 \cdot r}$ _____

6) $\sqrt{c^2 \cdot 16}$ _____

7) $\sqrt{red \cdot blue}$ _____

8) $\sqrt{foot \cdot hand}$ _____

9) $\sqrt{☆ \cdot ⊙}$ _____

10) $\sqrt{☹ \cdot △}$ _____

_____ %

Simplify these terms by splitting the squares.

See ASG, p. 129

1) $\sqrt{8}$ _____

2) $\sqrt{12}$ _____

3) $\sqrt{18}$ _____

4) $\sqrt{20}$ _____

5) $\sqrt{32}$ _____

6) $\sqrt{45}$ _____

7) $\sqrt{50}$ _____

8) $\sqrt{52}$ _____

9) $\sqrt{60}$ _____

10) $\sqrt{63}$ _____

11) $\sqrt{72}$ _____

12) $\sqrt{75}$ _____

13) $\sqrt{80}$ _____

14) $\sqrt{90}$ _____

15) $\sqrt{96}$ _____

16) $\sqrt{98}$ _____

17) $\sqrt{128}$ _____

18) $\sqrt{135}$ _____

19) $\sqrt{136}$ _____

20) $\sqrt{200}$ _____

21) $\sqrt{144b^2}$ _____

22) $\sqrt{81m^2s^2}$ _____

23) $\sqrt{64q^2}$ _____

24) $\sqrt{121a^2}$ _____

25) $\sqrt{36x^2}$ _____

26) $\sqrt{9y^2k^2}$ _____

27) $\sqrt{169w^2}$ _____

28) $\sqrt{100e^2f^2}$ _____

29) $\sqrt{196n^2t^2}$ _____

30) $\sqrt{49r^2}$ _____

31) $\sqrt{32w^2}$ _____

32) $\sqrt{12g^2}$ _____

33) $\sqrt{80v^2}$ _____

34) $\sqrt{45r^2p^2}$ _____

35) $\sqrt{75k^2q^2}$ _____

36) $\sqrt{63b^2c}$ _____

37) $\sqrt{18xy^2}$ _____

38) $\sqrt{96u}$ _____

39) $\sqrt{64r}$ _____

40) $\sqrt{81s^2}$ _____

41) $\sqrt{a^2b^2x}$ _____

42) $\sqrt{mp^2}$ _____

43) $\sqrt{36xy^2}$ _____

44) $\sqrt{w^2td^2}$ _____

45) $\sqrt{81ab^2c^2}$ _____

46) $\sqrt{8w^2z^2}$ _____

47) $\sqrt{20e^2m^2}$ _____

48) $\sqrt{75p^2r^2q}$ _____

49) $\sqrt{64t^2a^2}$ _____

50) $\sqrt{216n^2s^2tv}$ _____

_____ %

True or false?

See ASG, p. 130

1) $\sqrt{72} = \sqrt{9} \cdot \sqrt{8}$ _____

2) $\sqrt{9 \cdot 10} = \sqrt{9} + \sqrt{10}$ _____

3) $\sqrt{13 - 5} = \sqrt{13} - \sqrt{5}$ _____

4) $\sqrt{18bx} = \sqrt{18} \cdot \sqrt{b} \cdot \sqrt{x}$ _____

5) $\sqrt{100 + 64} = \sqrt{100} + \sqrt{64}$ _____

6) $\sqrt{m + x} = \sqrt{m} + \sqrt{x}$ _____

7) $\sqrt{8 \cdot 12} = \sqrt{8} \cdot \sqrt{12}$ _____

8) $\sqrt{30} = \sqrt{5} \cdot \sqrt{6}$ _____

9) $\sqrt{44} = \sqrt{22} + \sqrt{22}$ _____

10) $\sqrt{10 \cdot 10} = \sqrt{10} \cdot \sqrt{10}$ _____

_____ %

Simplify.

See ASG, p. 131

1) $\sqrt{8^2}$ _____

2) $\sqrt{15^2}$ _____

3) $\sqrt{b^2}$ _____

4) $\sqrt{w^2}$ _____

5) $\sqrt{(4m)^2}$ _____

6) $\sqrt{(13a)^2}$ _____

7) $\sqrt{(hat)^2}$ _____

8) $\sqrt{(glove)^2}$ _____

9) $\sqrt{\square^2}$ _____

10) $\sqrt{\diamond^2}$ _____

_____ %

Use the complex product radical rule to simplify these terms.

See ASG, p. 132

1) $3\sqrt{2} \cdot 4\sqrt{3}$ _____

2) $5\sqrt{5} \cdot 7\sqrt{3}$ _____

3) $a\sqrt{x} \cdot b\sqrt{y}$ _____

4) $m\sqrt{w} \cdot u\sqrt{v}$ _____

5) $8\sqrt{c} \cdot 3\sqrt{e}$ _____

6) $k\sqrt{5} \cdot n\sqrt{8}$ _____

7) $3\sqrt{tic} \cdot 6\sqrt{tac}$ _____

8) $7\sqrt{hot} \cdot 8\sqrt{cold}$ _____

9) $3\sqrt{\diamond} \cdot 4\sqrt{\triangledown}$ _____

10) $8\sqrt{\square} \cdot 6\sqrt{\triangle}$ _____

_____ %

Simplify these terms using the radical product shortcut.

See ASG, p. 133

1) $(4\sqrt{2})^2$ _____

2) $(6\sqrt{3})^2$ _____

3) $(7\sqrt{5})^2$ _____

4) $(3\sqrt{6})^2$ _____

5) $(y\sqrt{a})^2$ _____

6) $(b\sqrt{x})^2$ _____

7) $(5\sqrt{c})^2$ _____

8) $(6\sqrt{w})^2$ _____

9) $(v\sqrt{5})^2$ _____

10) $(p\sqrt{10})^2$ _____

_____ %

Use the radical quotient rule to simplify these terms.

See ASG, p. 134

1) $\dfrac{\sqrt{18}}{\sqrt{6}}$ _____

2) $\dfrac{\sqrt{a}}{\sqrt{c}}$ _____

3) $\dfrac{\sqrt{6m}}{\sqrt{8n}}$ _____

4) $\dfrac{\sqrt{arm}}{\sqrt{leg}}$ _____

_____ %

Simplify the following terms using the radical quotient rule.   See ASG, p. 135

1) $\dfrac{\sqrt{80}}{\sqrt{5}}$ _____

2) $\dfrac{\sqrt{54}}{\sqrt{6}}$ _____

3) $\dfrac{\sqrt{180}}{\sqrt{5}}$ _____

4) $\dfrac{\sqrt{28}}{\sqrt{7}}$ _____

5) $\dfrac{\sqrt{x^7}}{\sqrt{x^5}}$ _____

6) $\dfrac{\sqrt{m^7}}{\sqrt{m^3}}$ _____

7) $\dfrac{\sqrt{36a^3}}{\sqrt{4a}}$ _____

8) $\dfrac{\sqrt{320w^6}}{\sqrt{5w^2}}$ _____

_____ %

Split these radicals using the reverse radical quotient rule.   See ASG, p. 136

1) $\sqrt{\dfrac{8}{15}}$ _____

2) $\sqrt{\dfrac{m}{n}}$ _____

3) $\sqrt{\dfrac{mind}{matter}}$ _____

4) $\sqrt{\dfrac{\odot}{\bigstar}}$ _____

_____ %

Use the reverse radical quotient rule to simplify these terms.   See ASG, p. 137

1) $\sqrt{\dfrac{9}{25}}$ _____

2) $\sqrt{\dfrac{25}{36}}$ _____

3) $\sqrt{\dfrac{81}{100}}$ _____

4) $\sqrt{\dfrac{121}{196}}$ _____

5) $\sqrt{\dfrac{m^2}{y^2}}$ _____

6) $\sqrt{\dfrac{x}{16}}$ _____

7) $\sqrt{\dfrac{r^2}{15}}$ _____

8) $\sqrt{\dfrac{c^2}{144}}$ _____

_____ %

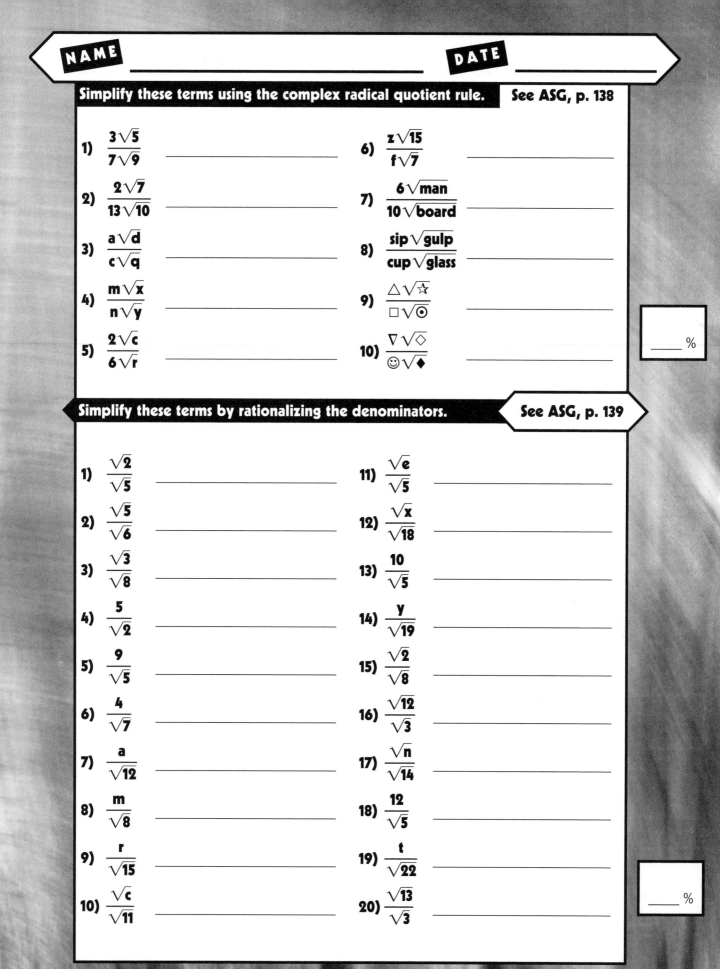

NAME _____ DATE _____

Simplify these terms using the complex radical quotient rule. See ASG, p. 138

1) $\dfrac{3\sqrt{5}}{7\sqrt{9}}$ _____

2) $\dfrac{2\sqrt{7}}{13\sqrt{10}}$ _____

3) $\dfrac{a\sqrt{d}}{c\sqrt{q}}$ _____

4) $\dfrac{m\sqrt{x}}{n\sqrt{y}}$ _____

5) $\dfrac{2\sqrt{c}}{6\sqrt{r}}$ _____

6) $\dfrac{z\sqrt{15}}{f\sqrt{7}}$ _____

7) $\dfrac{6\sqrt{\text{man}}}{10\sqrt{\text{board}}}$ _____

8) $\dfrac{\text{sip}\sqrt{\text{gulp}}}{\text{cup}\sqrt{\text{glass}}}$ _____

9) $\dfrac{\triangle\sqrt{\star}}{\square\sqrt{\odot}}$ _____

10) $\dfrac{\nabla\sqrt{\diamond}}{\smiley\sqrt{\blacklozenge}}$ _____

_____ %

Simplify these terms by rationalizing the denominators. See ASG, p. 139

1) $\dfrac{\sqrt{2}}{\sqrt{5}}$ _____

2) $\dfrac{\sqrt{5}}{\sqrt{6}}$ _____

3) $\dfrac{\sqrt{3}}{\sqrt{8}}$ _____

4) $\dfrac{5}{\sqrt{2}}$ _____

5) $\dfrac{9}{\sqrt{5}}$ _____

6) $\dfrac{4}{\sqrt{7}}$ _____

7) $\dfrac{a}{\sqrt{12}}$ _____

8) $\dfrac{m}{\sqrt{8}}$ _____

9) $\dfrac{r}{\sqrt{15}}$ _____

10) $\dfrac{\sqrt{c}}{\sqrt{11}}$ _____

11) $\dfrac{\sqrt{e}}{\sqrt{5}}$ _____

12) $\dfrac{\sqrt{x}}{\sqrt{18}}$ _____

13) $\dfrac{10}{\sqrt{5}}$ _____

14) $\dfrac{y}{\sqrt{19}}$ _____

15) $\dfrac{\sqrt{2}}{\sqrt{8}}$ _____

16) $\dfrac{\sqrt{12}}{\sqrt{3}}$ _____

17) $\dfrac{\sqrt{n}}{\sqrt{14}}$ _____

18) $\dfrac{12}{\sqrt{5}}$ _____

19) $\dfrac{t}{\sqrt{22}}$ _____

20) $\dfrac{\sqrt{13}}{\sqrt{3}}$ _____

_____ %

Are these terms in their original or factored forms?

See ASG, p. 142

1) 15 _____
2) $3x^2$ _____
3) $4 \cdot 5$ _____
4) $8 \cdot (p - 4)$ _____

5) 16xyz _____
6) $7r \cdot 3s$ _____
7) $4m^2n$ _____
8) $4p \cdot (t + 7)$ _____

_____ %

Identify the coefficient.

See ASG, pp. 143–144

1) 3mn _____
2) wv^2 _____
3) $(2/7)pqr$ _____
4) $-b^2c^2$ _____

5) $-4x^2$ _____
6) x^2y _____
7) $-efg$ _____
8) 1.63k _____

_____ %

Tell whether these are monomials, binomials, or trinomials.

See ASG, p. 146

1) $-4p^2$ _____
2) $m^6 + 3m^2$ _____
3) $-3x^2 - x + 2$ _____
4) $2y + 3$ _____
5) $6.3a^2 - 1.2a$ _____

6) mp _____
7) $b^2 + 16b + 4$ _____
8) $-6/13$ _____
9) $c^6 + 5c^4 - 4c^2$ _____
10) $2 + 3w$ _____

_____ %

List all the factors of these numbers.

See ASG, p. 148

1) 4 _____
2) 6 _____
3) 10 _____
4) 12 _____
5) 20 _____
6) 21 _____
7) 25 _____
8) 28 _____
9) 36 _____
10) 40 _____

11) 45 _____
12) 60 _____
13) 75 _____
14) 85 _____
15) 96 _____
16) 100 _____
17) 121 _____
18) 125 _____
19) 144 _____
20) 200 _____

_____ %

List the primary factors of these monomials.

See ASG, p. 149

1) $12p^2$ _____

2) $8xyz$ _____

3) $15b^2c$ _____

4) $13w^2v^2$ _____

5) $16pq^2$ _____

_____ %

Find the GCF for these sets of numbers.

See ASG, p. 151

1) 35, 49, 56 _____

2) 15, 21, 27 _____

3) 14, 42, 56 _____

4) 36, 60, 72 _____

5) 36, 54, 90 _____

6) 40, 64, 88 _____

7) 27, 81, 135 _____

8) 40, 60, 70 _____

9) 40, 60, 80 _____

10) 69, 115, 161 _____

_____ %

Find the GCF for these groups of monomials.

See ASG, p. 152

1) $3m, 6m, 9m$ _____

2) $5x, 10, 15x$ _____

3) $8b, 12b^2, 16b^2$ _____

4) $2y, 5y, 9y$ _____

5) $14ac, 56c^2, 28a^2c$ _____

6) $6p^2r, 12p^2, 24p^2r^2$ _____

7) $8a^3x^5, 17ax^2, 9a^2x$ _____

8) $12mnp, 18mp, 30n$ _____

9) $20xy, 30x^2y^2, 50xy^2$ _____

10) $24b^3c^2, 40b^2c^3, 72b^4c^5$ _____

11) $35x^2y^2z^2, 63x^4yz^3, 49x^3y^2z$ _____

12) $6a^3b^4, 36a^2b^3c, 54ab^2c^3$ _____

13) $18d^2f^2, 26ef^2, 34d^3e^2$ _____

14) $17x^2y^2, 11xz^3, 23yz^2$ _____

15) $18ck^2p, 45k^2p, 72ck^2$ _____

_____ %

Factor these polynomials.

See ASG, p. 153

1) $12m^2 + 4m$ _____

2) $15k^3 - 10k^2$ _____

3) $7x - 28x^2$ _____

4) $18 + 6w^3$ _____

5) $24x^2 + 18x^3$ _____

6) $16a^2c - 24ac^2$ _____

7) $18m^2np + 30np^2$ _____

8) $6rv^2u - 4mpv^2$ _____

9) $14w^2xy - 21wxy$ _____

10) $4a^2b^2c^2 + 8abc$ _____

11) $12d^2 - 8d - 4$ _____

12) $15r^3 + 5r^2 - 10r$ _____

13) $6xy^2 - 18xy - 12x$ _____

14) $14a^2b + 28ab^2 + 42ab$ _____

15) $5x^2 - 7x^3 + 12x^4$ _____

16) $6m^2np^2 - 15mn^2p^2 + 9mnp^3$ _____

17) $81r^2t^3 - 63r^2t^2 + 36r^2t$ _____

18) $81u^3v^4 + 27u^3v^3 - 54u^3$ _____

19) $6c^2e - 8c^2e^2 - 12c^3e$ _____

20) $36p^2q^3 + 44p^3q^3 + 28p^2q^2$ _____

_____ %

Tell whether or not each of these is a quadratic trinomial.

See ASG, p. 154

1) $x^3 + x^2 - 5$ _____

2) $a + 5$ _____

3) $d^2 - 2d + 4$ _____

4) $m^3 + 8m + 1$ _____

5) $3b^2 - 4b + 5$ _____

6) $5n^3 + 6n^2 - 1$ _____

7) $2y^4 - 3y + 9$ _____

8) $c - c^2 + 5$ _____

9) $-8r^2 + 3r + 2$ _____

10) $3 + t^3 - t$ _____

11) $p^2 - 3p - 18$ _____

12) $2t^7 + t^2 + 1$ _____

13) $5x + x^2 + 3x^3$ _____

14) $5 + e^2 - 2e$ _____

15) $-9u^2 + 6u + 3$ _____

16) $6s - 5s^4 + 1$ _____

17) $v + 6v^2 + 9$ _____

18) $3 - m + 4m^5$ _____

19) $2t^2 + 3t - 12$ _____

20) $w - 14 - 6w^2$ _____

_____ %

Write the pairs of factors whose product is the given number. See ASG, p. 156

1) + 4 _____
2) – 4 _____
3) + 6 _____
4) – 6 _____
5) + 8 _____
6) – 8 _____
7) + 14 _____
8) – 14 _____
9) + 24 _____
10) – 24 _____
11) + 27 _____
12) – 27 _____
13) + 30 _____
14) – 30 _____
15) + 48 _____

_____ %

Find the appropriate pair of factors. See ASG, p. 157

1) What pair of factors of + 4 add up to + 4? _____
2) What pair of factors of – 4 add up to – 3? _____
3) What pair of factors of + 6 add up to – 7? _____
4) What pair of factors of – 6 add up to + 1? _____
5) What pair of factors of + 8 add up to – 6? _____
6) What pair of factors of – 8 add up to – 7? _____
7) What pair of factors of + 14 add up to + 9? _____
8) What pair of factors of – 14 add up to – 13? _____
9) What pair of factors of + 24 add up to + 14? _____
10) What pair of factors of – 24 add up to + 5? _____
11) What pair of factors of + 27 add up to + 12? _____
12) What pair of factors of – 27 add up to – 6? _____
13) What pair of factors of + 30 add up to – 11? _____
14) What pair of factors of – 30 add up to + 7? _____
15) What pair of factors of + 48 add up to + 14? _____

_____ %

Factor these + + + trinomials.   See ASG, p. 158

1) $c^2 + 4c + 3$ _____
2) $m^2 + 5m + 6$ _____
3) $w^2 + 6w + 8$ _____
4) $x^2 + 7x + 6$ _____
5) $e^2 + 7e + 10$ _____
6) $m^2 + 7m + 12$ _____
7) $t^2 + 8t + 7$ _____
8) $u^2 + 9u + 18$ _____
9) $y^2 + 9y + 20$ _____
10) $x^2 + 10x + 9$ _____
11) $a^2 + 10a + 21$ _____
12) $b^2 + 11b + 18$ _____
13) $p^2 + 11p + 24$ _____
14) $m^2 + 11m + 28$ _____
15) $r^2 + 11r + 30$ _____

16) $p^2 + 12p + 27$ _____
17) $x^2 + 12x + 32$ _____
18) $m^2 + 13m + 22$ _____
19) $q^2 + 13q + 30$ _____
20) $c^2 + 13c + 36$ _____
21) $e^2 + 13e + 40$ _____
22) $r^2 + 13r + 42$ _____
23) $x^2 + 14x + 45$ _____
24) $b^2 + 14b + 48$ _____
25) $n^2 + 15n + 56$ _____
26) $p^2 + 16p + 48$ _____
27) $s^2 + 16s + 60$ _____
28) $x^2 + 17x + 60$ _____
29) $k^2 + 18k + 72$ _____
30) $c^2 + 20c + 75$ _____

_____ %

Factor these + – + trinomials.   See ASG, p. 159

1) $x^2 - 4x + 3$ _____
2) $b^2 - 4b + 4$ _____
3) $z^2 - 5z + 4$ _____
4) $u^2 - 5u + 6$ _____
5) $y^2 - 6y + 5$ _____
6) $w^2 - 6w + 8$ _____
7) $b^2 - 7b + 6$ _____
8) $k^2 - 7k + 10$ _____
9) $d^2 - 7d + 12$ _____
10) $w^2 - 13w + 30$ _____
11) $x^2 - 13x + 36$ _____
12) $m^2 - 32m + 60$ _____
13) $e^2 - 23e + 60$ _____
14) $g^2 - 17g + 60$ _____
15) $f^2 - 16f + 60$ _____

16) $k^2 - 35k + 96$ _____
17) $s^2 - 28s + 96$ _____
18) $n^2 - 22n + 96$ _____
19) $p^2 - 20p + 96$ _____
20) $x^2 - 29x + 100$ _____
21) $t^2 - 12t + 27$ _____
22) $u^2 - 12u + 35$ _____
23) $q^2 - 15q + 36$ _____
24) $v^2 - 15v + 50$ _____
25) $z^2 - 15z + 56$ _____
26) $r^2 - 18r + 45$ _____
27) $y^2 - 18y + 72$ _____
28) $a^2 - 18a + 80$ _____
29) $c^2 - 21c + 90$ _____
30) $d^2 - 21d + 110$ _____

_____ %

Factor these + + − trinomials.

See ASG, p. 160

1) $m^2 + 6m - 27$ _____

2) $b^2 + 6b - 40$ _____

3) $a^2 + 6a - 55$ _____

4) $z^2 + 3z - 18$ _____

5) $y^2 + 3y - 28$ _____

6) $c^2 + 3c - 40$ _____

7) $r^2 + 3r - 54$ _____

8) $f^2 + f - 12$ _____

9) $p^2 + p - 20$ _____

10) $x^2 + 12x - 28$ _____

11) $d^2 + 3d - 28$ _____

12) $w^2 + 18w - 40$ _____

13) $b^2 + 39b - 40$ _____

14) $e^2 + 19e - 42$ _____

15) $k^2 + 12k - 45$ _____

16) $v^2 + 4v - 45$ _____

17) $g^2 + 45g - 144$ _____

18) $f^2 + 32f - 144$ _____

19) $k^2 + 18k - 144$ _____

20) $u^2 + 10u - 144$ _____

21) $m^2 + 10m - 39$ _____

22) $t^2 + 10t - 96$ _____

23) $p^2 + 10p - 200$ _____

24) $m^2 + 12m - 28$ _____

25) $n^2 + 12n - 64$ _____

26) $d^2 + 12d - 108$ _____

27) $q^2 + 12q - 160$ _____

28) $c^2 + 15c - 16$ _____

29) $r^2 + 15r - 154$ _____

30) $s^2 + 15s - 250$ _____

_____ %

Factor these + − − trinomials.

See ASG, p. 161

1) $k^2 - 5k - 14$ _____

2) $h^2 - 5h - 24$ _____

3) $m^2 - 5m - 50$ _____

4) $x^2 - 8x - 84$ _____

5) $y^2 - 8y - 128$ _____

6) $z^2 - 8z - 33$ _____

7) $a^2 - 11a - 26$ _____

8) $n^2 - 11n - 60$ _____

9) $b^2 - 12b - 45$ _____

10) $z^2 - 12z - 28$ _____

11) $p^2 - 9p - 36$ _____

12) $m^2 - 5m - 36$ _____

13) $f^2 - 16f - 36$ _____

14) $q^2 - 7q - 30$ _____

15) $c^2 - 13c - 30$ _____

16) $e^2 - e - 30$ _____

17) $d^2 - 20d - 21$ _____

18) $r^2 - 4r - 21$ _____

19) $c^2 - 12c - 85$ _____

20) $d^2 - 84d - 85$ _____

21) $s^2 - 14s - 15$ _____

22) $b^2 - 14b - 51$ _____

23) $e^2 - 14e - 120$ _____

24) $t^2 - 17t - 38$ _____

25) $a^2 - 17a - 110$ _____

26) $f^2 - 24f - 112$ _____

27) $u^2 - 6u - 112$ _____

28) $g^2 - 54g - 112$ _____

29) $v^2 - 124v - 125$ _____

30) $w^2 - 20w - 125$ _____

_____ %

Identify the terms.

See ASG, p. 162

For the expression $(+x+5)(+x-3)$, which terms are the

1) Firsts? _____

2) Outers? _____

3) Inners? _____

4) Lasts? _____

For the expression $(+a-2)(+a+6)$, which terms are the

5) Firsts? _____

6) Outers? _____

7) Inners? _____

8) Lasts? _____

_____ %

F.O.I.L. these binomials.

See ASG, p. 163

1) $(k+2)(k+3)$ _____

2) $(m+1)(m+5)$ _____

3) $(v+4)(v+6)$ _____

4) $(d+8)(d-3)$ _____

5) $(u+3)(u+9)$ _____

6) $(t+5)(t-9)$ _____

7) $(e-10)(e+2)$ _____

8) $(w+6)(w+1)$ _____

9) $(f+8)(f-9)$ _____

10) $(x-11)(x-3)$ _____

11) $(g-15)(g-6)$ _____

12) $(c+19)(c-3)$ _____

13) $(s-14)(s-10)$ _____

14) $(b+13)(b-6)$ _____

15) $(n-18)(n-8)$ _____

16) $(x+5)(x-15)$ _____

17) $(c-9)(c+13)$ _____

18) $(t+16)(t+3)$ _____

19) $(r-11)(r-13)$ _____

20) $(d+5)(d-19)$ _____

21) $(h-7)(h+14)$ _____

22) $(k+12)(k+18)$ _____

23) $(v-21)(v-2)$ _____

24) $(u+13)(u-14)$ _____

25) $(z-8)(z+11)$ _____

26) $(p-16)(p-9)$ _____

27) $(a+15)(a-8)$ _____

28) $(q-11)(q+17)$ _____

29) $(r-13)(r-12)$ _____

30) $(y-20)(y-17)$ _____

_____ %

Factor these expressions.

See ASG, p. 165

1) x^2-25 _____

2) m^2-49 _____

3) k^2-100 _____

4) w^2-144 _____

5) $4c^2-36$ _____

6) $9w^2-64$ _____

7) $25y^2-25$ _____

8) $16c^2-4$ _____

9) $36n^2-1$ _____

10) $4p^2-9r^2$ _____

11) $9x^2y^2-16z^2$ _____

12) a^2-b^2 _____

13) $n^2p^2-4v^2$ _____

14) $25-x^2$ _____

15) $81-1$ _____

_____ %

Cancel and reduce these fractions.

See ASG, p. 169

1) 8m/8 _____

2) 3/3p _____

3) 6/6xy _____

4) 12a/12 _____

5) 5r/5 _____

6) 16ce/16 _____

7) 7/7k _____

8) $20/20p^2$ _____

_____ %

List the terms you can cancel in these fractions.

See ASG, p. 171

1) $\dfrac{ab}{a}$ _____

2) $\dfrac{3xy}{3y}$ _____

3) $\dfrac{c(m + n)}{d(m + n)}$ _____

4) $\dfrac{ax(p + q)}{bx(p - q)}$ _____

5) $\dfrac{xyz}{xy}$ _____

6) $\dfrac{m(n + p)}{mnp}$ _____

7) $\dfrac{ek}{e(w + r)}$ _____

8) $\dfrac{br(s + t)}{xm(s + t)}$ _____

9) $\dfrac{wcq}{c(w - q)}$ _____

10) $\dfrac{vn(c + d)}{avn(c - d)}$ _____

_____ %

Cancel and give the simplified form of these terms.

See ASG, p. 172

1) $\dfrac{ab}{a}$ _____

2) $6 - \dfrac{x}{x}$ _____

3) $\dfrac{3mn}{mn}$ _____

4) $\dfrac{p}{q} + \dfrac{q}{q}$ _____

5) $9 - \dfrac{cd}{c}$ _____

6) $\dfrac{5yz}{5z}$ _____

7) $\dfrac{a(b + c)}{3a}$ _____

8) $\dfrac{u}{v} + \dfrac{v}{v}$ _____

9) $7x - \dfrac{y}{y}$ _____

10) $\dfrac{rmq}{q}$ _____

_____ %

Good news! Not only can you factor variable terms, you can also factor numbers. For example, in a problem like $\frac{4 + 8x}{4}$, you can factor 4 out of the numerator to get $\frac{4(1 + 2x)}{4}$. Then you can cancel the 4s to get $1 + 2x$ as the final answer. And in the same way, in $\frac{5 + 15x}{10}$, you can factor 5 out of the two terms in the numerator, to get $\frac{5(1 + 3x)}{10}$. Then you can cancel the 5 in the numerator with the 10 in the denominator, to get $\frac{1 + 3x}{2}$ as the final answer.

NEW CONCEPT!

Simplify these fractions using the F.C.R. steps.

See ASG, p. 174

1) $\dfrac{6x + 12y}{6}$ _____

2) $\dfrac{ab + ac}{a}$ _____

3) $\dfrac{9m + 15n}{6}$ _____

4) $\dfrac{16}{8u - 24v}$ _____

5) $\dfrac{10s - 25t}{5}$ _____

6) $\dfrac{m}{me + mv}$ _____

7) $\dfrac{14w}{7x + 21y}$ _____

8) $\dfrac{12d - 8e + 20f}{4}$ _____

9) $\dfrac{12p - 36q}{24}$ _____

10) $\dfrac{15n + 6r - 18k}{9}$ _____

_____ %

More good news! You can factor numbers out of both the numerator and denominator. For example, in a problem like $\frac{4 + 8x}{8 - 12x}$, you can factor 4 out of both the numerator and denominator, to get $\frac{4(1 + 2x)}{4(2 - 3x)}$. Then you can cancel both 4s to get $\frac{1 + 2x}{2 - 3x}$ as the final answer.

You can even factor different numbers from numerator and denominator. For example, in $\frac{5 + 15x}{10 - 30x}$, you can factor a 5 out of the numerator, to get $5(1 + 3x)$. Then you can factor a 10 out of the denominator, to get $10(1 - 3x)$. Finally, you can cancel the 5 in the numerator with the 10 in the denominator, to get a final answer of $\frac{1 + 3x}{2(1 - 3x)}$.

NEW CONCEPT!

Reduce these fractions using the F.C.R. steps.

See ASG, p. 175

1) $\dfrac{3m + 3n}{6b + 6c}$ _____

2) $\dfrac{3 - 6y}{6 - 9y}$ _____

3) $\dfrac{7d + 21f}{14d - 21f}$ _____

4) $\dfrac{12n - 4r}{6n + 4r}$ _____

5) $\dfrac{8 + 10e}{12 + 18e}$ _____

6) $\dfrac{10 - 15m}{10m + 40}$ _____

7) $\dfrac{8a - 16c}{8a - 12c}$ _____

8) $\dfrac{2rv - 4sq}{6xy + 8wz}$ _____

9) $\dfrac{6nr + 12st}{9ns + 15rt}$ _____

10) $\dfrac{4x + 6z}{6z - 8x}$ _____

_____ %

You can simplify fractions even they have factors that are variables. For example, in the problem $\frac{3x^2 + 6x^4}{12x^3 - 4x}$, first factor the GCF in the numerator and denominator, to get $\frac{3x^2(1 + 2x^2)}{4x(3x^2 - 1)}$. Then cancel the x terms to get the final answer: $\frac{3x(1 + 2x^2)}{4(3x^2 - 1)}$.

NEW CONCEPT!

Reduce these fractions.   See ASG, p. 176

1) $\dfrac{6g^3 - 12g}{2g^3 + 2g^2}$ _____

2) $\dfrac{9y^2 - 6y}{6y^3 + 15y^2}$ _____

3) $\dfrac{4c^2 + 8c^4}{8c^3 - 2c}$ _____

4) $\dfrac{6n^3 + 9n^2}{6n^5 + 6n^3}$ _____

5) $\dfrac{12r^2 - 16r^3}{10r^2 + 30r^4}$ _____

6) $\dfrac{4a^2b + 12ab}{2ab}$ _____

7) $\dfrac{t^4 - 3t^3}{t^2}$ _____

8) $\dfrac{18u^2 - 24u^3}{6u}$ _____

9) $\dfrac{6z^3 - 9z^2}{3z^2}$ _____

10) $\dfrac{4c^3d - 6cd^2}{2cd}$ _____

_____ %

Is "x" a factor of these expressions?   See ASG, p. 177

1) $4x$ _____

2) $x + y$ _____

3) $4 + x$ _____

4) $x(5 + a)$ _____

5) $y(x + z)$ _____

6) $x - (2 + x)$ _____

7) $ax(a - x)$ _____

8) $x(x + 2)$ _____

9) $vw(x - v)$ _____

10) $vx(v - w)$ _____

_____ %

Name the factor(s) of the numerator and denominator.   See ASG, p. 178

1) $\dfrac{5(d + g)}{15(d + g)}$ _____

2) $\dfrac{n(r + t)}{r + t}$ _____

3) $\dfrac{9(e + f)}{12e}$ _____

4) $\dfrac{n + p - r}{r(n + p)}$ _____

5) $\dfrac{s - t + v}{t + v}$ _____

6) $\dfrac{x - y}{w(x - y)}$ _____

7) $\dfrac{6m^2}{(u + m)}$ _____

8) $\dfrac{4(p - q)}{6(p + q)}$ _____

9) $\dfrac{3(b + c)}{(b + c)^2}$ _____

10) $\dfrac{x^2(y - z)}{(y^2 - z^2)}$ _____

_____ %

Reduce these fractions.
(Careful! You may need to factor and cancel first.)

See ASG, p. 179

1) $\dfrac{a + b}{2(a + b)}$ _____

2) $\dfrac{3(x + y)}{5(x + y)}$ _____

3) $\dfrac{m - n}{m - n}$ _____

4) $\dfrac{p + r + t}{3(p + r + t)}$ _____

5) $\dfrac{3u(v + z)}{2w(v + z)}$ _____

6) $\dfrac{9(k - 3)}{k - 3}$ _____

7) $\dfrac{s + 1}{6s + 6}$ _____

8) $\dfrac{dx + ex}{dy + ey}$ _____

9) $\dfrac{3u + 6}{7u^2 + 14u}$ _____

10) $\dfrac{4ac - 4c}{2ad^2 - 2d^2}$ _____

_____ %

Use the split-the-numerator rule, but don't simplify further.

See ASG, p. 181

1) $\dfrac{x + y}{z}$ _____

2) $\dfrac{a + b - 3}{c}$ _____

3) $\dfrac{n^2 - r}{r}$ _____

4) $\dfrac{ant - mouse}{spider}$ _____

5) $\dfrac{11 - t}{21}$ _____

6) $\dfrac{p + 2}{z}$ _____

7) $\dfrac{\bullet + \odot}{\bigstar}$ _____

8) $\dfrac{c + d}{2}$ _____

9) $\dfrac{3v + 2u - 4x}{2x}$ _____

10) $\dfrac{k^2 - 4k}{4}$ _____

_____ %

Simplify these fractions using the split-the-numerator rule.

See ASG, p. 183

1) $\dfrac{4 + d}{d}$ _____

2) $\dfrac{c + e}{c}$ _____

3) $\dfrac{x - y}{x^2}$ _____

4) $\dfrac{p^2 - q}{q}$ _____

5) $\dfrac{a + b^2}{b^2}$ _____

6) $\dfrac{n - r^2}{r}$ _____

7) $\dfrac{v + k + w}{v}$ _____

8) $\dfrac{u + t + s}{s}$ _____

9) $\dfrac{x^2 - y^2}{x^2}$ _____

10) $\dfrac{a + b - c}{a}$ _____

_____ %

Identify the parts of these equations.

See ASG, p. 191

$$10y - 9 = 41 + 8y \qquad 8z - 3 = 4z + 9 - 12z$$

1) $10y - 9$ _____
2) $+41$ _____
3) $+8y$ _____
4) $41 + 8y$ _____
5) y _____

6) -3 _____
7) $8z - 3$ _____
8) $4z$ _____
9) z _____
10) $4z + 9 - 12z$ _____

_____ %

Work through the simplifying phase for these equations. (You will work more with these equations on the following two pages.)

See ASG, p. 193

1) $2(a - 4) + 3a = 3a - 2$ _____
2) $4(k - 4) = 8(k + 1)$ _____
3) $4p - (p - 15) = 6(10 - p) + 4p$ _____
4) $3(b + 3) + 4b + 8 = 4(b + 8)$ _____
5) $28 - 5e = 4(10 - 3e) + 6e$ _____
6) $5(m + 4) = 2(m + 2) + 4$ _____
7) $-2(q + 8) + 2(4q - 3) = 2(4q + 3)$ _____
8) $4(3 - c) + 5c + 3 = 6c - 20$ _____
9) $6(f + 1) - 3(f + 2) = 3(2f + 3) + 6$ _____
10) $4(n - 5) + 3n - 6 = 3(n + 2)$ _____
11) $3(d - 3) - 2(1 - 3d) = 6d - 5$ _____
12) $3(r + 5) + 2(r - 2) = 2(r - 9) - 1$ _____
13) $8(s + 1) + 4s + 6 = 6(s + 3) + 2$ _____
14) $10(v - 7) + 5(4v - 6) = 26v$ _____
15) $2(5y - 2) - 22 = 11y - (3y + 6)$ _____
16) $25 - t = 46 + 3t - 3(12 + t)$ _____
17) $2(w + 17) + 5w - 1 = 2(w + 2) + 3(w + 5)$ _____
18) $4(z - 5) + 5 = -9(z + 3) + z$ _____
19) $4u - 3(u - 7) = 3(u + 11) + 3(u + 9) - 2u$ _____
20) $6(-x - 4) - 18x + 12 = 3(14 - 11x)$ _____

_____ %

Solve these mini-equations.

See ASG, p. 195

1) $x + 4 = 9$ _____

2) $b + 4 = 12$ _____

3) $r + 6 = 3$ _____

4) $v + 18 = 11$ _____

5) $n - 3 = 4$ _____

6) $d - 10 = -15$ _____

7) $k - 6 = 12$ _____

8) $t - 2 = 13$ _____

9) $4 \cdot e = 24$ _____

10) $-5 \cdot q = 20$ _____

11) $8 \cdot m = -48$ _____

12) $-3 \cdot w = -21$ _____

13) $y/7 = 5$ _____

14) $f/4 = 3$ _____

15) $c/6 = -10$ _____

16) $-s/8 = 6$ _____

17) $a^2 = 36$ _____

18) $p^2 = 121$ _____

19) $u^2 = 4$ _____

20) $z^3 = 27$ _____

_____ %

Now work through the isolating phase for these equations.

See ASG, p. 197

1) $5a - 8 = 3a - 2$ _____

2) $9d - 11 = 6d - 5$ _____

3) $4k - 16 = 8k + 8$ _____

4) $3p + 15 = 60 - 2p$ _____

5) $7b + 17 = 4b + 32$ _____

6) $28 - 5e = 40 - 6e$ _____

7) $5m + 20 = 2m + 8$ _____

8) $6q - 22 = 8q + 6$ _____

9) $c + 15 = 6c - 20$ _____

10) $3f = 6f + 15$ _____

11) $7n - 26 = 3n + 6$ _____

12) $5r + 11 = 2r - 19$ _____

13) $12s + 14 = 6s + 20$ _____

14) $30v - 100 = 26v$ _____

15) $10y - 26 = 8y - 6$ _____

16) $25 - t = 10$ _____

17) $7w + 33 = 5w + 19$ _____

18) $4z - 15 = -8z - 27$ _____

19) $u + 21 = 4u + 60$ _____

20) $-24x - 12 = 42 - 33x$ _____

_____ %

Finally, work through the solving phase for these equations.   See ASG, p. 198

1) $2a = 6$ _____
2) $3d = 6$ _____
3) $-24 = 4k$ _____
4) $5p = 45$ _____
5) $3b = 15$ _____
6) $-e = -12$ _____
7) $-12 = 3m$ _____
8) $28 = -2q$ _____
9) $5c = 35$ _____
10) $3f = -15$ _____

11) $4n = 32$ _____
12) $-30 = 3r$ _____
13) $6s = 6$ _____
14) $4v = 100$ _____
15) $20 = 2y$ _____
16) $-t = -15$ _____
17) $2w = -14$ _____
18) $12z = -12$ _____
19) $-39 = 3u$ _____
20) $9x = 54$ _____

_____ %

Work through the S.I.S. phases to solve these equations.   See ASG, p. 199

1) $3(2a - 5) = 2(a + 10) - 15$ _____
2) $4(e + 3) + 12e = 5(e + 4) + 7(e + 5) + 5$ _____
3) $2(r + 3) = 3(4 - r) - 11$ _____
4) $2(n - 7) + 6n = 6(n + 2)$ _____
5) $2(3 - b) - 2b = 6(-b + 2) - 26$ _____
6) $5f + 4 = 5(f - 3) + 4f + 3$ _____
7) $-6(k - 7) + 3k = 2(k - 4)$ _____
8) $6(p + 10) - 3(2p + 12) = -4p + 4$ _____
9) $3(c + 3) + 6c = 3(c + 7) + 3(c + 4) - 3$ _____
10) $6(d + 6) - 8 = 2(d + 30)$ _____
11) $4(m + 5) + 4 = m + 6$ _____
12) $2(8 - q) + 5q = 5(q + 5) + 1$ _____
13) $8v + 40 = 2(3v + 10) - 2$ _____
14) $5(z + 10) + 10 = 12(z + 2) - 10z$ _____
15) $2(u - 13) = 4(16 - u)$ _____
16) $4s - 3(s + 4) = 2(2s + 3) + 9$ _____
17) $6(5 - w) = 2(w + 5) + 4$ _____
18) $2(2 - x) + 3x = 2(x + 12)$ _____
19) $4(18 - y) + 18 = 12(3 + y) - 7y$ _____
20) $5(t + 19) + 10 = 6(t + 9) - 4t$ _____

_____ %

Solve these equations.

See ASG, p. 200

1) $q/4 + 10 = 3 \cdot 5$ _____

2) $6 - r/2 = 10 - 8$ _____

3) $2(6 - 3) = (v + 5)/4$ _____

4) $5(a/3) = 2(3 + 2)$ _____

5) $p/5 = 5 - 3 \cdot 2$ _____

6) $10 - n/5 = 3 \cdot 4 - 5$ _____

7) $b/7 + 6 = 9 - 5$ _____

8) $t/3 - 7 = -10 + 2 \cdot 3$ _____

9) $-4 + u/2 = 8/4$ _____

10) $5(c/2) = -14 + 4$ _____

11) $e/2 + 7 = 4e$ _____

12) $2m - m/7 = 6 + m$ _____

13) $2x + 15 = x/2 - 3$ _____

14) $-4 + d/4 = d + 2$ _____

15) $y/5 + 3 = y/2$ _____

_____ %

Solve these equations.

See ASG, p. 201

1) $2n^2 - 9 = n^2$ _____

2) $a^2 + 4 = 13 + 7$ _____

3) $2g^2 = 4(17 + 8) + g^2$ _____

4) $p^2 - 9 = 8 \cdot 5$ _____

5) $4b^2 = 30 + 7(6 + 4)$ _____

6) $20 \cdot 5 - 19 = r^2$ _____

7) $z^2 - 5 \cdot 25 = 10^2$ _____

8) $18 + 2x^2 = 2(9 \cdot 5)$ _____

9) $5(14 + 5) = s^2 - 7^2$ _____

10) $(3c^2)/2 = 3(98)$ _____

11) $4v^2 - 64 = 3v^2$ _____

12) $-d^2 + 200 = d^2 - 42$ _____

13) $2(t^2 + 3) = t^2 + 55$ _____

14) $5 \cdot 5 = e^2/4$ _____

15) $u^2 - 9 = (24/25)u^2$ _____

_____ %

Solve — or begin solving — these absolute value equations.

See ASG, p. 202

1) $|m| = 5$ _____

2) $|n| = 8$ _____

3) $|3r - 4| = 13$ _____

4) $|10 - y| = 1$ _____

_____ %

Solve these absolute value equations.

See ASG, p. 203

1) $|2a - 3| = 9$ _____

2) $|1 - 3k| = 10$ _____

3) $|2n + 5| = 3$ _____

4) $|6(b + 1)| = 18$ _____

5) $|4r + 6| = 10$ _____

6) $|12 - 3e| = 6$ _____

7) $|8c - 3| = 5$ _____

8) $|10 - 5t| = 15$ _____

9) $|2d + 2| = d + 10$ _____

10) $|4p - 6| = p + 9$ _____

_____ %

Solve these quadratic trinomials equations.

See ASG, pp. 204–205

1) $v^2 + 6v + 8 = 0$ _____

2) $m^2 - 4m - 12 = 0$ _____

3) $u^2 - 10u + 21 = 0$ _____

4) $t^2 + 4t - 32 = 0$ _____

5) $s^2 + 8s + 15 = 0$ _____

6) $x^2 - 4x - 45 = 0$ _____

7) $k^2 - 9k + 20 = 0$ _____

8) $c^2 + 5c - 84 = 0$ _____

9) $r^2 + 7r + 6 = 0$ _____

10) $y^2 - 9y - 22 = 0$ _____

11) $w^2 - 15w + 54 = 0$ _____

12) $p^2 + 6p - 7 = 0$ _____

13) $z^2 + 12z + 32 = 0$ _____

14) $q^2 + 8q - 20 = 0$ _____

15) $n^2 - 10n - 75 = 0$ _____

_____ %

Find the length of the hypotenuse of each right triangle (round to the tenths place, if necessary).

See ASG, p. 209

1) legs have lengths 2 cm. and 6 cm. _____

2) legs have lengths 4 inches and 10 inches _____

3) legs have lengths 5 miles and 12 miles _____

4) legs have lengths 7 feet and 24 feet _____

5) legs have lengths 9 meters and 15 meters _____

6) legs have lengths 7 inches and 18 inches _____

7) legs have lengths 5 feet and 21 feet _____

8) legs have lengths 9 yards and 40 yards _____

9) legs have lengths 11 lightyears and 60 lightyears _____

10) legs have lengths 10 mm. and 23 mm. _____

_____ %

Find the length of the second leg of each right triangle (round to the tenths place, if necessary).

See ASG, p. 210

1) leg = 2 yards, hypotenuse = 3 yards _____

2) leg = 4 meters, hypotenuse = 5 meters _____

3) leg = 5 feet, hypotenuse = 13 feet _____

4) leg = 6 cm., hypotenuse = 9 cm. _____

5) hypotenuse = 17 mm., leg = 10 mm. _____

6) hypotenuse = 25 inches, leg = 7 inches _____

7) hypotenuse = 10 feet, leg = 6 feet _____

8) leg = 9 miles, hypotenuse = 41 miles _____

9) hypotenuse = 16 yards, leg = 12 yards _____

10) leg = 7 meters, hypotenuse = 9 meters _____

_____ %

Graph these points on two sets of coordinate axes. See ASG, p. 218

COORDINATE PLANE A

A) (-3, 4)
B) (4, -5)
C) (5, 2)
D) (2, 4)
E) (-2, -3)
F) (0, 1)
G) (-1, 2)
H) (-5, -2)
J) (1, -3)
K) (-4, 1)

COORDINATE PLANE B

A) (2, -4)
B) (-8, -2)
C) (4, 6)
D) (6, -8)
E) (-3, 5)
F) (0, -6)
G) (-10, -7)
H) (5, 2)
J) (10, -7)
K) (-1, 9)

_____ %

State the values for x_1, y_1, x_2, and y_2. See ASG, p. 221

1) P_1 is (6, -8), P_2 is (7, -4) _____

2) P_1 is (1, 4), P_2 is (-5, -6) _____

3) P_1 is (3, -7), P_2 is (3, 11) _____

4) P_1 is (5, 2), P_2 is (9, 2) _____

5) P_1 is (6, 9), P_2 is (12, -4) _____

6) P_1 is (7, -1), P_2 is (-6, 14) _____

7) P_1 is (4, 6), P_2 is (1, -3) _____

8) P_1 is (-2, 1), P_2 is (2, 6) _____

9) P_1 is (-3, -8), P_2 is (4, -9) _____

10) P_1 is (0, 4), P_2 is (-6, -10) _____

_____ %

Find the slope of the line passing through these points. See ASG, p. 222

1) $(4, 2)$ and $(8, 4)$ _____

2) $(9, 1)$ and $(6, 4)$ _____

3) $(3, -1)$ and $(7, 0)$ _____

4) $(-4, -2)$ and $(-2, 2)$ _____

5) $(5, 3)$ and $(-1, 9)$ _____

6) $(-4, 2)$ and $(-2, 10)$ _____

7) $(7, 8)$ and $(8, 11)$ _____

8) $(0, -2)$ and $(10, -6)$ _____

9) $(-3, 3)$ and $(-4, 13)$ _____

10) $(0, 1)$ and $(1, 2)$ _____

_____ %

Given one point (P_1) and the slope (m), graph the lines on two coordinate planes. See ASG, pp. 224–225

COORDINATE PLANE A

a) $P_1 = (-4, 4)$, $m = 1$

b) $P_1 = (6, 4)$, $m = 1/2$

c) $P_1 = (-4, -6)$, $m = 3/4$

d) $P_1 = (5, -2)$, $m = 1/5$

e) $P_1 = (0, 3)$, $m = 2/3$

COORDINATE PLANE B

f) $P_1 = (0, 0)$, $m = 2$

g) $P_1 = (-3, 4)$, $m = 1/4$

h) $P_1 = (2, -5)$, $m = 2/5$

j) $P_1 = (-9, -5)$, $m = 3/4$

k) $P_1 = (-6, 0)$, $m = 7$

_____ %

Given one point (P_1) and the slope (m), graph the lines on two coordinate planes. See ASG, pp. 226–227

COORDINATE PLANE C

l) $P_1 = (1, 3)$, $m = -1/3$

m) $P_1 = (-5, 1)$, $m = -3$

n) $P_1 = (8, -8)$, $m = -2/5$

p) $P_1 = (3, -2)$, $m = -3/4$

q) $P_1 = (-7, -6)$, $m = -1/6$

COORDINATE PLANE D

r) $P_1 = (-3, 4)$, $m = -5/3$

s) $P_1 = (7, 6)$, $m = -1/6$

t) $P_1 = (-5, -6)$, $m = -10$

u) $P_1 = (9, -6)$, $m = -2/3$

v) $P_1 = (-2, -4)$, $m = -1/7$

_____ %

Name the x- and y-intercepts for each of these lines.   See ASG, p. 229

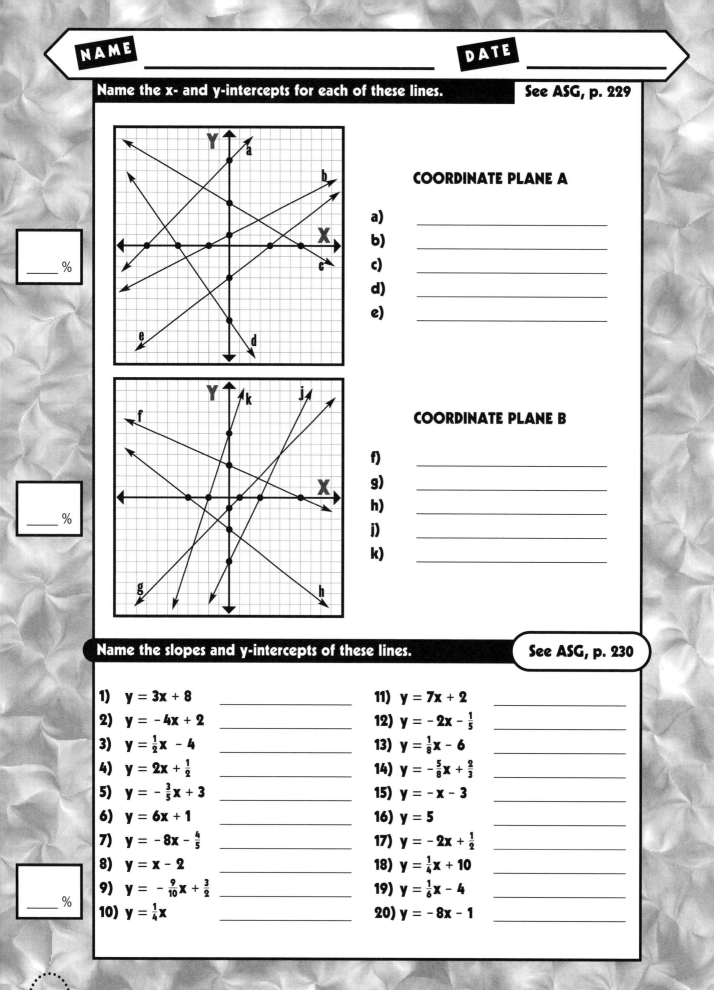

_____ %

COORDINATE PLANE A

a) _____
b) _____
c) _____
d) _____
e) _____

_____ %

COORDINATE PLANE B

f) _____
g) _____
h) _____
j) _____
k) _____

Name the slopes and y-intercepts of these lines.   See ASG, p. 230

1) $y = 3x + 8$ _____

2) $y = -4x + 2$ _____

3) $y = \frac{1}{2}x - 4$ _____

4) $y = 2x + \frac{1}{2}$ _____

5) $y = -\frac{3}{5}x + 3$ _____

6) $y = 6x + 1$ _____

7) $y = -8x - \frac{4}{5}$ _____

8) $y = x - 2$ _____

9) $y = -\frac{9}{10}x + \frac{3}{2}$ _____

10) $y = \frac{1}{4}x$ _____

11) $y = 7x + 2$ _____

12) $y = -2x - \frac{1}{5}$ _____

13) $y = \frac{1}{8}x - 6$ _____

14) $y = -\frac{5}{8}x + \frac{2}{3}$ _____

15) $y = -x - 3$ _____

16) $y = 5$ _____

17) $y = -2x + \frac{1}{2}$ _____

18) $y = \frac{1}{4}x + 10$ _____

19) $y = \frac{1}{6}x - 4$ _____

20) $y = -8x - 1$ _____

_____ %

Graph these lines on four coordinate planes. See ASG, pp. 231–232

a) $y = 3x$	d) $y = \frac{1}{2}x - 2$
b) $y = \frac{1}{3}x + 2$	e) $y = -\frac{2}{3}x + 1$
c) $y = -\frac{3}{2}x - 5$	f) $y = \frac{4}{5}x + 3$
g) $y = \frac{3}{4}x + 4$	k) $y = \frac{1}{2}x + 5$
h) $y = 6x + 4$	l) $y = \frac{1}{2}x + 1$
j) $y = -\frac{1}{4}x + 4$	m) $y = \frac{1}{2}x - 4$

_____ %

Given one point (P_1) and the slope (m), write the equation of the line. See ASG, p. 233

1) $P_1 = (2, 4)$, m = 2 _____

2) $P_1 = (2, -7)$, m = 3/5 _____

3) $P_1 = (5, 8)$, m = 1/2 _____

4) $P_1 = (-3, 8)$, m = -1 _____

5) $P_1 = (9, 12)$, m = 1/3 _____

6) $P_1 = (-8, -2)$, m = 2 _____

7) $P_1 = (-4, 6)$, m = -3 _____

8) $P_1 = (-1, 7)$, m = 2/9 _____

9) $P_1 = (5, -10)$, m = -2 _____

10) $P_1 = (0, -3)$, m = 5/8 _____

_____ %

Given two points, write the equation of the line. See ASG, p. 234

1) $(4, -7)$ and $(8, -1)$ _____

2) $(6, -3)$ and $(-3, 15)$ _____

3) $(6, 3)$ and $(8, 0)$ _____

4) $(3, -4)$ and $(9, 2)$ _____

5) $(15, 3)$ and $(5, -1)$ _____

6) $(-2, 10)$ and $(5, -25)$ _____

7) $(1, 12)$ and $(-2, -12)$ _____

8) $(-1, 4)$ and $(-5, 7)$ _____

9) $(4, 10)$ and $(-2, -8)$ _____

10) $(-3, 7)$ and $(-5, 2)$ _____

_____ %

Write these equations in slope-intercept form. See ASG, p. 235

1) $-6x + 3y = 18$ _____

2) $16 + 2y = 6x$ _____

3) $14 - 7y = 21x$ _____

4) $5x - 5y = 10$ _____

5) $3y + 6x = 4$ _____

6) $9 - 4y - 2x = 1$ _____

7) $7y + 5x = 5$ _____

8) $6x - y = 10$ _____

9) $12 + 3y = 8x$ _____

10) $6y - 36 = 9x$ _____

11) $15x - 21 = 5y$ _____

12) $3(x + y) = 9$ _____

13) $8x = 5(y + 2)$ _____

14) $9y - 3x + 3 = 0$ _____

15) $14x + 3y = -15$ _____

16) $2 + 3y = 11 - x$ _____

17) $3x + y = 5x - 4$ _____

18) $7y - 5 = 3x + 2y$ _____

19) $8(x - 2) = 3(x + 2y)$ _____

20) $4(x - y) = 7(x + 2) - y$ _____

_____ %

Write the equations of these lines, then graph them on two coordinate planes. See ASG, p. 236

COORDINATE PLANE A

a) the vertical line through $(4, 0)$ _____

b) the horizontal line through $(-3, 2)$ _____

c) the vertical line through $(-6, 3)$ _____

d) the horizontal line through $(-3, -3)$ _____

COORDINATE PLANE B

e) the horizontal line through $(-6, 3)$ _____

f) the vertical line through $(2, 4)$ _____

g) the horizontal line through $(5, -2)$ _____

h) the vertical line through $(-3, -5)$ _____

_____ %

Solve these pairs of equations (find the intersection point). See ASG, pp. 238–239

1) $2y + 2x = 6$
   $y + 6x = -7$ _____

2) $5y + 8 = 2x$
   $2x + y = 20$ _____

3) $5x - 3 = 4y$
   $2y + 3x = -7$ _____

4) $3y = x - 18$
   $y + 4x = 7$ _____

5) $y + 2x = -4$
   $y + 9 = 3x$ _____

6) $y = 2x + 6$
   $y + 10 = 4x$ _____

7) $3x + 2y = 9$
   $2x + 3y = 6$ _____

8) $x - 8y = 4$
   $4y + 4x = 52$ _____

9) $6x + 2 = y$
   $4y - 3x = -34$ _____

10) $2x + 3y = 6$
    $2y - x = 4$ _____

11) $3y + x = -4$
    $y + 2x = 2$ _____

12) $3x + 2y = 18$
    $7x + 3y = 32$ _____

13) $y - 2x = 9$
    $3y + 6 = -5x$ _____

14) $y = 2x + 25$
    $3y + x = 5$ _____

15) $3y - 7x = 15$
    $x - 3y = 3$ _____

16) $2y = x + 16$
    $5y + 2x = 40$ _____

17) $2y + 7x = -32$
    $3x - 12 = 2y$ _____

18) $y + 18 = 3x$
    $5y + 3x = 0$ _____

19) $9x - 2y = 7$
    $y + 2x = 16$ _____

20) $y + 3 = 4x$
    $4y + x = 22$ _____

_____ %

**Solve each pair of equations to find the intersection point.
Then graph the lines to confirm that they intersect there.** See ASG, p. 240

1) $x + y = 1$
   $2y - x = 8$ _____

2) $y - x = -1$
   $y - 2x = -2$ _____

3) $y - 3x = 3$
   $y + 2x = -2$ _____

4) $3y - x = 6$
   $x - y = 0$ _____

5) $5x - 2y = 12$
   $3x + 2y = 4$ _____

6) $x - y = 2$
   $2x + y = -8$ _____

7) $5y - 3x = 10$
   $5y - 2x = 15$ _____

8) $2y - x = 12$
   $4x + y = -3$ _____

9) $y - 3x = 2$
   $3y + x = 6$ _____

10) $6x + y = -3$
    $y - 2x = 5$ _____

_____ %

Find the distance between each pair of points.   See ASG, p. 242

1) (5, 5) and (2, 1) _____
2) (3, 8) and (8, -4) _____
3) (2, -8) and (-5, -16) _____
4) (10, 8) and (6, 2) _____
5) (2, 6) and (-1, 1) _____

6) (5, 3) and (7, -3) _____
7) (5, -2) and (-1, -10) _____
8) (-3, -7) and (-1, 0) _____
9) (-5, -4) and (3, 7) _____
10) (5, 7) and (-4, -5) _____

_____ %

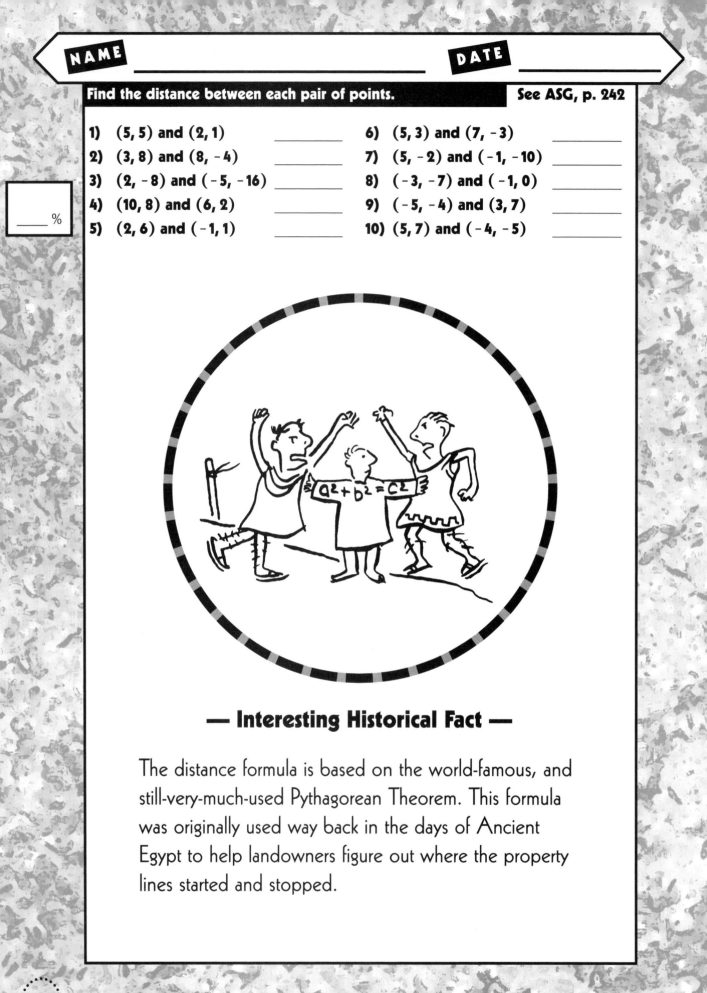

— **Interesting Historical Fact** —

The distance formula is based on the world-famous, and still-very-much-used Pythagorean Theorem. This formula was originally used way back in the days of Ancient Egypt to help landowners figure out where the property lines started and stopped.

Write these phrases using algebraic symbols.   See ASG, pp. 248–249

1)   Four less than a number.   _____

2)   Eight more than a number.   _____

3)   Eighteen more than a number.   _____

4)   Eighteen less than a number.   _____

5)   Sixty less than a number.   _____

6)   Three times a number.   _____

7)   Seven less than the opposite of a number.   _____

8)   Six times the opposite of a number.   _____

9)   Three times the quantity of five less than three times a number.   _____

10) Ten more than four times the opposite of a number.   _____

11) The opposite of the quantity of three less than two times a number.   _____

12) Nine less than six times a number.   _____

13) Nine less than six times the opposite of a number.   _____

14) Six times the quantity of nine less than a number.   _____

15) Nine times the quantity of six less than three times a number.   _____

_____ %

Translate these statements into equations, but don't solve them.   See ASG, p. 250

1)   Eight more than a number equals three times the number.   _____

2)   What percent of twenty is nine?   _____

3)   The sum of two consecutive integers is fifteen.   _____

4)   What percent of forty is ten?   _____

5)   Three times the quantity of two more than a number is twenty-one.   _____

6)   Two times the quantity of six less than a number equals the opposite of the number.   _____

7)   Nine is thirty percent of what number?   _____

8)   A number equals three times the quantity of five less than twice the number.   _____

9)   The opposite of the quantity of one more than two times a number equals five.   _____

10) The sum of three consecutive integers is thirty-three.   _____

11) Six times a number divided by five equals two more than the number.   _____

12) What percent of eighty is sixteen?   _____

13) The sum of four consecutive integers is eighteen.   _____

14) The opposite of four times a number equals ten more than the number.   _____

15) Thirty divided by a number equals one less than the number.   _____

_____ %

Solve for the variable in these word problems.

See ASG, p. 251

1) Two more than three times a number equals eleven. _____

2) Five times the quantity of one less than two times a number equals twenty-five. _____

3) Thirteen times a number equals four times the quantity of five more than two times the number. _____

4) Four times the quantity of six more than twice a number equals twice the number. _____

5) Three more than two times a number equals six more than the opposite of the number. _____

6) Six more than four times a number equals eight less than three times the number. _____

7) Four times the quantity of eight less than the opposite of a number is three more than three times the number. _____

8) Seven times the quantity of twenty less than four times a number is eight times the number. _____

9) Five times the quantity of six less than a number is two times the quantity of three more than the number. _____

10) Four less than ten times a number is fourteen times the number. _____

_____ %

Solve these percent word problems.

See ASG, p. 252

1) What percent of 60 is 12? _____   6) What percent of 40 is 36? _____

2) What percent of 50 is 5? _____   7) 76 is what percent of 100? _____

3) 4 is what percent of 200? _____   8) 54 is what percent of 27? _____

4) What percent of 56 is 14? _____   9) What percent of 5 is 2? _____

5) 45 is what percent of 36? _____   10) 24 is what percent of 30? _____

_____ %

Solve these percent increase problems.

See ASG, p. 253

1) What's the result when 75 is increased by 20%? _____

2) What's the result when 60 is increased by 30%? _____

3) 40 gets increased by 5%. What's the result? _____

4) What's the result when 12 is increased by 50%? _____

5) 2 gets increased by 50%. What's the result? _____

6) What's the result when 15 is increased by 200%? _____

7) What's the result when 56 is increased by 25%? _____

8) 300 gets increased by 45%. What's the result? _____

9) What's the result when 120 is increased by 70%? _____

10) 80 gets increased by 35%. What's the result? _____

_____ %

Solve these consecutive integer problems.

See ASG, p. 254

1) Two consecutive integers add up to 9. What are they? _____

2) Two consecutive even integers add up to 26. What are they? _____

3) Three consecutive integers add up to 24. What are they? _____

4) Three consecutive even integers add up to 30. What are they? _____

5) Four consecutive integers add up to 54. What are they? _____

6) Two consecutive odd integers add up to 76. What are they? _____

7) Four consecutive even integers add up to 52. What are they? _____

8) Three consecutive odd integers add up to 129. What are they? _____

9) Five consecutive integers add up to 85. What are they? _____

10) Four consecutive odd integers add up to 64. What are they? _____

_____ %

Solve these age problems.

See ASG, p. 256

1) Eli is three years older than Jon. Two years ago, Eli's age was four times Jon's age. How old is Eli now? _____

2) Chris is five times as old as Zac. In thirty years, Chris will be twice Zac's age. How old is Zac now? _____

3) Dawn is four years younger than Melanie. Five years ago, Melanie was twice Dawn's age. How old is Melanie now? _____

4) Paul is six years older than Corinne. Ten years ago, twice Paul's age was triple Corinne's age. How old is Paul now? _____

5) Debbie is 16 years younger than Asher. Three years from now, Asher will be three times as old as Debbie. How old is Asher now? _____

_____ %

Solve for the third quantity.

See ASG, p. 258

1) $r = 15$ mph; $t = 3$ hours _____

2) $t = 2$ hours; $d = 18$ miles _____

3) $d = 50$ miles; $r = 25$ mph _____

4) $t = 6$ hours; $d = 72$ miles _____

5) $r = 60$ mph; $t = 5$ hours _____

6) $d = 100$ miles; $t = 5$ hours _____

7) $t = 8$ hours; $r = 3$ mph _____

8) $r = 15$ mph; $d = 75$ miles _____

9) $d = 117$ miles; $t = 9$ hours _____

10) $r = 36$ mph; $d = 90$ miles _____

_____ %

Solve these $d_1 = d_2$ problems.

See ASG, pp. 260–261

1) Stacy rode her bike away from home for 3 hours at 8 miles per hour, but then she got a flat tire. Her dad drove out to pick her up, but it only took him 1 hour to get there. How fast did Stacy's dad drive? _____

2) Antoine drives from Chicago to Minneapolis to visit his aunt. He drives for 6 hours at 60 miles per hour. On the way home, bad weather forces him to drive 45 miles per hour. How long will the return trip take? _____

3) Esteban is a long-distance runner who runs for 5 hours at 9 kilometers per hour. Tony is a skateboarder who skates at 15 kilometers per hour. How long does it take Tony to cover the same distance? _____

4) Rachel skis down a mountain at 1500 feet per minute for 20 minutes. The ski lift takes 50 minutes to return her to the top. How fast does the ski lift travel? _____

5) Every day, Sisyphus is forced to roll a boulder up a mountain at 1 mile per hour for 16 hours. Every night, he slips at the top and the boulder rolls back down the mountain in 15 minutes (1/4 of an hour). How fast does the boulder roll down the hill? _____

_____%

Solve these $d_1 + d_2 = d_{total}$ problems.

See ASG, pp. 262–263

1) Sarah leaves her house on her bike, headed west at 8 miles per hour. Her brother, Mark, leaves on foot, headed east at 3 miles per hour. How far apart will they be after 4 hours? _____

2) Rebecca and Luke live 200 miles apart. If they leave their houses at the same time, Luke driving at 40 miles per hour and Sarah driving at 60 miles per hour, how long will it be until they meet? _____

3) Naomi leaves Dallas on a train heading north at 75 miles per hour. At the same time, John leaves Dallas on a train heading south. After three hours, they are 420 miles apart. How fast is John's train going? _____

4) Alex and Isabel leave St. Louis at the same time, heading in opposite directions. If Alex travels at 12 miles per hour and Isabel travels at 16 miles per hour, how many hours pass before they are 168 miles apart? _____

5) Jacob lives 18 miles away from Beth. They leave their houses at the same time, aiming to meet somewhere in between. If they end up meeting 6 miles from Beth's house after 2 hours, how fast does Jacob walk? _____

_____%

1)	Reflexive	1)	Distributive	1)	Multiplicative identity
2)	None	2)	Associative	2)	Additive identity
3)	Symmetric	3)	Commutative	3)	Multiplicative identity
4)	Transitive	4)	Distributive	4)	None
5)	None	5)	Commutative	5)	Additive identity
6)	Symmetric	6)	None	6)	None
7)	Transitive	7)	Distributive	7)	None
8)	None	8)	None	8)	None
9)	None	9)	Associative	9)	Multiplicative identity
10)	Symmetric	10)	Associative	10)	Additive identity

1)	N, W, I	11)	N, W, I	1)	R	11)	R
2)	I	12)	N, W, I	2)	I	12)	I
3)	N, W, I	13)	None	3)	I	13)	R
4)	W, I	14)	I	4)	R	14)	R
5)	I	15)	None	5)	I	15)	I
6)	None	16)	N, W, I	6)	R	16)	I
7)	I	17)	I	7)	R	17)	R
8)	N, W, I	18)	N, W, I	8)	I	18)	I
9)	None	19)	I	9)	R	19)	R
10)	None	20)	None	10)	R	20)	I

1)	+3	11)	+19	21)	+14	31)	+10	41)	+25
2)	+7	12)	−21	22)	+14	32)	−20	42)	+18
3)	−10	13)	−21	23)	−16	33)	−30	43)	+10
4)	+8	14)	+25	24)	+24	34)	+40	44)	−25
5)	−12	15)	+17	25)	−26	35)	+28	45)	−40
6)	−3	16)	−25	26)	−20	36)	−30	46)	+21
7)	+13	17)	+42	27)	+18	37)	−23	47)	+40
8)	+15	18)	−39	28)	+27	38)	+26	48)	−46
9)	−10	19)	−30	29)	+45	39)	+58	49)	+66
10)	−11	20)	+34	30)	−56	40)	−33	50)	−79

1)	+1	11)	−5	21)	−3	31)	−10	41)	+8	51)	−100	61)	−37
2)	+1	12)	+1	22)	−32	32)	+7	42)	+31	52)	+2	62)	−689
3)	−3	13)	+2	23)	−16	33)	+13	43)	−1	53)	+32	63)	−275
4)	+2	14)	−3	24)	−10	34)	−30	44)	+15	54)	−80	64)	−313
5)	+6	15)	−3	25)	+40	35)	+14	45)	+15	55)	+203	65)	+362
6)	−2	16)	−6	26)	+13	36)	+10	46)	+21	56)	+362	66)	+692
7)	+2	17)	+5	27)	+6	37)	+40	47)	−45	57)	+500	67)	+176
8)	+1	18)	+6	28)	−9	38)	−36	48)	+4	58)	−269	68)	+400
9)	+4	19)	+8	29)	+9	39)	−28	49)	−24	59)	+366	69)	+109
10)	+2	20)	+1	30)	−18	40)	+45	50)	+25	60)	+489	70)	−302

1) S, −10
2) M, − 4
3) S, +10
4) M, + 4
5) M, − 3
6) M, + 3
7) S, −13
8) S, +13
9) M, − 4
10) S, +13

11) M, + 7
12) S, +21
13) M, +13
14) S, − 20
15) S, +21
16) S, +45
17) M, − 10
18) M, + 8
19) M, − 3
20) M, + 4

1) + 3
2) + 4
3) − 5
4) 0
5) + 2
6) +15
7) − 44
8) +16
9) − 20
10) −16

11) + 36
12) + 16
13) − 80
14) + 30
15) + 30
16) − 41
17) − 35
18) +131
19) +448
20) − 288

1) +10
2) − 21
3) +27
4) − 60
5) − 45

1) − 5
2) + 6
3) +17
4) − 9
5) + 28

1) +37
2) + 3
3) + 4
4) − 31
5) +11
6) +14
7) +52
8) − 9
9) +56
10) − 54

11) +20
12) − 56
13) − 45
14) +24
15) − 49
16) +73
17) +76
18) − 91
19) +24
20) − 7

21) + 5
22) +73
23) − 79
24) − 23
25) +151
26) − 94
27) +27
28) +34
29) +122
30) − 25

1) − 3 − 2, S, − 5
2) − 8 + 5, M, − 3
3) + 7 + 4, S, +11
4) − 9 − 7, S, −16
5) + 6 − 7, M, − 1
6) + 8 + 4, S, +12
7) − 7 + 3, M, − 4
8) + 2 − 2, M, 0
9) − 1 + 8, M, + 7

10) − 4 − 6, S, −10
11) +12 + 8, S, +20
12) − 7 − 17, S, − 24
13) +24 − 9, M, +15
14) + 4 + 31, S, +35
15) − 46 − 8, S, − 54
16) +27 − 35, M, − 8
17) − 61 + 45, M, −16
18) − 86 − 52, S, −138

19) − 76 + 63, M, −13
20) +21 + 81, S, +102
21) −126 − 804, S, − 930
22) +312 − 392, M, − 80
23) +181 + 406, S, +587
24) − 240 − 376, S, − 616
25) +621 + 412, S, +1,033

1) − 11
2) − 7
3) − 1
4) 0
5) − 4
6) − 4
7) +11
8) + 7
9) − 2
10) − 4

11) − 3
12) − 37
13) − 81
14) − 99
15) +75
16) −129
17) +177
18) −126
19) − 83
20) −194

1) − 6
2) − 24
3) +56
4) − 52
5) +64
6) +48
7) − 448
8) +486
9) − 300
10) +68

1) -8
2) $+3$
3) -4
4) $+20/6$ or $+10/3$
5) $+5$
6) $+23$
7) $-19/4$
8) $+7$
9) -8
10) -9

1) Parentheses before exponents, $+81$
2) Parentheses before multiplication, $+18$
3) Exponents before mixed-sign rule, -12
4) Parentheses before exponents, $+4$
5) Exponents before multiplication, $+144$
6) Grouping before mixed-sign rule, -8
7) Division before same-sign rule, $+10$
8) Parentheses before mixed-sign rule, -2
9) Parentheses and exponents before mixed-sign rule, -20
10) Exponents before same-sign rule, $+40$

1) First (), then []
2) First (), then {}
3) First {}, then [], then ()
4) First (), then {}, then []
5) First (), then ||
6) First [], then (), then {}
7) First [], then (), then ||
8) First ||, then (), then {}
9) First ||, then {}, then []
10) First (), then [], then {}

1) 64
2) -38
3) 46
4) 3
5) -5
6) 13
7) -34
8) 49
9) 25
10) -5

11) -20
12) 9
13) 0
14) 43
15) 4
16) -2
17) -7
18) 4
19) -6
20) 15

1) 20
2) 20
3) 5
4) 5
5) 125
6) 125
7) 125
8) 9
9) 9
10) 4

11) 1
12) 42
13) 42
14) 42
15) 1
16) 16
17) 1
18) 1
19) 9
20) 1/4

1) 18
2) 16
3) 32
4) 36
5) 48
6) 144
7) 225
8) 28
9) 98
10) 100

1a) 36
2a) 64
3a) 64
4a) 144
5a) 144
6a) 72
7a) 45
8a) 196
9a) 196
10a) 20

1) -4
2) -9
3) -16
4) -25
5) -36
6) 49
7) 64
8) -81
9) 100
10) -121

1a) 4
2a) 9
3a) 16
4a) 25
5a) 36
6a) -49
7a) -64
8a) 81
9a) -100
10a) 121

1) Yes
2) No
3) No
4) Yes
5) No
6) Yes
7) No
8) Yes
9) Yes
10) No

1) $5m$
2) q
3) rmx
4) $3ab$
5) $2c^2d$
6) mr
7) $2z^2$
8) $2t^2v$
9) 0
10) $5x^2z$

1) $6a$
2) $5x$
3) $4m$
4) $5r$
5) $3c$
6) $6y$
7) 0
8) f
9) $5r^2$
10) $2mn$

For example, 4 apples + 2 apples = 6 apples
For example, 3 eggs + 2 eggs = 5 eggs
For example, 6 monkeys − 2 monkeys = 4 monkeys
For example, 4 rhinos + 1 rhino = 5 rhinos
For example, 5 cats − 2 cats = 3 cats
For example, 4 yolks + 1 yolk + 1 yolk = 6 yolks
For example, 2 babies − 2 babies = 0 babies
For example, 6 frogs − 3 frogs − 2 frogs = 1 frog
For example, 2 rats + 3 rats = 5 rats
For example, 4 men − 2 men = 2 men

1) +10x
2) −19y
3) +26m
4) −22a
5) −28q

1) −5n
2) −9p
3) −5c
4) +13d
5) −7r

1) +19f
2) −15x
3) −4c
4) −28h
5) −5e
6) +5d
7) +21w
8) −8x
9) +17v
10) −27b

11) −9d
12) −37a
13) +15z
14) +7m
15) −32r
16) +41u
17) +23t
18) −31q
19) −15c
20) +2m

21) −11b
22) +45s
23) −37p
24) +9k
25) +46h
26) −40n
27) −9a
28) +16j
29) +42g
30) −7y

page 18

1) 3mn
2) −3mq
3) −8rx
4) −bcx
5) $2rx^2$
6) $−3dq^2$
7) 2mp
8) 0
9) 2fv
10) −3gh

11) 6pt
12) r^2nw
13) −4qx
14) $3b^2c$
15) −2def
16) $2r^2nz$
17) 0
18) $3.1p^2$
19) $−28pqr^2$
20) $2bdf^2$

1) 3x + 2y
2) 2
3) −q + 4
4) 6bc + df
5) −xz + 2
6) −hn − bq
7) −3m + 5.2
8) $2y^2 − 2y$
9) $8cd^2 − 2f$
10) $4xy + \frac{1}{3}$

11) 3np − 2pr
12) 0
13) 6qh − 3qt
14) 6p
15) 4ty − 4
16) $4r^2 − 2pr$
17) $5n^2x + 4.3$
18) 4xy + 3yz
19) $−7r^2 − 2mt$
20) $5r^2qb + 2rqb$

page 19

1) a + b
2) a − b
3) −a − b
4) −a + b
5) −y − 6
6) y − 6
7) y + 6
8) −y + 6
9) −3 − g
10) −6 + m

11) −3 + x
12) −n − p − 2
13) p + r − 3
14) −a + b + c
15) 2 − q
16) m − n + p
17) −d − e + 6
18) x + y + z
19) p − q − r
20) a + 4 − c

1) a + 5
2) 1 − b
3) c + 3
4) d + 3
5) e − 3
6) −f
7) −g − 4
8) −h − 2
9) j − 1
10) k − 18

11) −m
12) n + 15
13) p + 15
14) 3 − q
15) r − 10
16) −s − 3
17) t
18) −u − 15
19) 4 − v
20) −w

page 20

1) 4
2) 4
3) 2/3
4) 42
5) 1.6
6) 7.25
7) 7.25
8) 5/6
9) 5/6
10) 9

1) 2
2) 20
3) 20
4) 12
5) 6
6) 6
7) 2
8) 0
9) 12
10) 24

1) 7
2) −1
3) 4
4) 3
5) −3
6) 6
7) 6
8) −6
9) 10
10) 2

11) −3
12) −10
13) 12
14) 0
15) −4

1) -6
2) 3
3) 16
4) -2
5) -5
6) -50
7) 3
8) 24
9) -1
10) 9

11) 10
12) -13
13) 144
14) 4
15) -14
16) 36
17) -16
18) 5
19) 3
20) -25

1) 5
2) -8
3) -9
4) 7
5) 9
6) 7
7) -2
8) 1
9) 2
10) -2

1) 9
2) $n \cdot n$
3) $n \cdot n \cdot n$
4) 8
5) $(4x) \cdot (4x) = 16x^2$
6) 27
7) $b \cdot b \cdot b$
8) 64
9) $(pq) \cdot (pq) = p^2q^2$
10) $\left(\dfrac{1}{4}\right) \cdot \left(\dfrac{1}{4}\right) = \dfrac{1}{16}$

1) 3^{10}
2) w^8
3) 4^{m+n}
4) 6^6
5) aardvark^7
6) p^9
7) 4^{11}
8) $2^{hip+hop}$
9) r^{12}
10) 6^{x+y}

11) 10^{20}
12) a^{15}
13) $\triangle^{15}$
14) c^{15}
15) 12^{10}
16) t^{5n}
17) a^{b+c}
18) $\diamond^9$
19) 87^{36}
20) $(xy)^{w+z}$

1) 3^4
2) w^4
3) 5^4
4) $\bullet^5$
5) 8^{a-b}
6) a^8
7) $\text{tic}^{tac-toe}$
8) $(p+q)^{r-s}$
9) $\heartsuit^7$
10) $m^{d-d} = m^0 = 1$

1) $8y^2$
2) $42p^3$
3) $6m^4$
4) $25b^7$
5) $32x^5$
6) $12v^2$
7) $12t^9$
8) $12a^{10}$
9) $54f$
10) $50c^6$

11) $40w$
12) $15e^4$
13) $4y^2$
14) $24p^4$
15) $30x^6$

1) $2m$
2) $3r^2$
3) $4p^3$
4) $5q^4$
5) $3m^8$
6) 2
7) e^2
8) y
9) $\frac{3}{2}t^4$
10) 1

11) $6p^{x-y}$
12) $7d^8$
13) $2c^5$
14) $2x^6$
15) $4d^3$

1) 3
2) 1
3) 1
4) -10
5) 1
6) π
7) 1
8) 12
9) 162
10) 1

1) a^4
2) 5
3) 11
4) x^2y^4
5) $a+2$
6) mn^2
7) $4mn^2$
8) $r^2 - 1$
9) $\dfrac{a^3b^2c}{xz^4}$
10) $5/9$

1) $y - 3$
2) $y^2 + 2y - 6$
3) $-m^2 - m + 3$
4) $2b^3 + 3b^2 - 3b - 4$
5) $n^2 + 13$
6) $2c^2 - c + 3$
7) $-2p^4 - 3p^3 + p^2 + 6p + 9$
8) $x^5 - 3x + 7$
9) $a^3 - 2a^2 + 9a - 5$
10) $3e^2 - 2e + 5$

11) $8r^4 - 3r^3 + r^2 - r + 4$
12) $12t^3 + 2t^2 - t + 5$
13) $-3q^2 - 5q + 5$
14) $8w^5 + 3w^4 - 4w^3 - 2w^2 - w + 6$
15) $-s^3 - s^2 + s + 5$

1) $1/x^2$
2) $1/b^4$
3) $1/c^8$
4) $1/\diamond^5$
5) $1/81$
6) $1/7^n$
7) $1/12^{earring}$
8) $1/y^x$
9) $1/cat^{dog}$
10) $1/8^m$

1) 2^7
2) p^6
3) 3^x
4) $\oplus^w$
5) $ski^{snowboard}$
6) r^6
7) 8^c
8) $pizza^{slice}$
9) $\diamondsuit^3$
10) 7

1) $\dfrac{3}{x^2 y^3}$
2) $\dfrac{x^3}{y^2}$
3) $\dfrac{2m^2 r^3}{5n^4 p^4}$
4) $7a^2 b^3 c^5$

5) $\dfrac{e^3}{d^2}$
6) $\dfrac{r^2 j^8}{f^3 x^5}$
7) $\dfrac{6p^2}{r^2}$
8) $\dfrac{36n^2 x^3 r^2}{p^4 m^2}$

9) $\dfrac{25xy^2 n^2}{9m^3}$
10) $\dfrac{d^x e^y f^z}{a^n b^m c^p}$

1) 2^4
2) x^7
3) $\dfrac{1}{4^3}$
4) $\dfrac{1}{clone^5}$
5) m^8

6) z^{13}
7) $\dfrac{1}{10^8}$
8) $lemur^3$
9) $\dfrac{1}{r}$
10) $\dfrac{1}{n^7}$

1) $\dfrac{1}{r^9}$
2) m^5
3) $\dfrac{1}{3^{24}}$
4) x
5) eel^{13}
6) $\dfrac{4^2}{z^{18}} = \dfrac{16}{z^{18}}$

6) c^{20}
7) $\dfrac{1}{z^5}$
8) $\dfrac{1}{pony^{11}}$
9) 6^5
10) $\dfrac{1}{v}$

1) $\dfrac{a^6}{b}$
2) $\dfrac{r^6}{3^1} = \dfrac{r^6}{3}$
3) $4^1 w^8 = 4w^8$
4) $\dfrac{v^6}{t^2}$
5) $\dfrac{1}{8^2 n^7} = \dfrac{1}{64n^7}$

6) 1
7) $5^3 d^7 = 125d^7$
8) $\dfrac{1}{9^2 z^{11}} = \dfrac{1}{81z^{11}}$
9) $\dfrac{u^6}{k^5}$
10) $7^1 = 7$

1) 3^8
2) a^{15}
3) c^{xy}
4) 4^6
5) $llama^{16}$
6) k^{-8}
7) $\odot^{30}$
8) p^{-xz}
9) gum^{36}
10) n^{24}

11) 6^{10}
12) 12^{-18}
13) $\diamond^{cf}$
14) 3^{27}
15) p^{4r}
16) 8^{-48}
17) v^{20}
18) $\star^{-vw}$
19) e^{-28}
20) bug^{-3d}

1) e^9
2) $2^3 p^9 = 8p^9$
3) x^5
4) $(-2)^2 r^6 = 4r^6$
5) $\dfrac{1}{b^5}$
6) $\dfrac{4^2}{z^{18}} = \dfrac{16}{z^{18}}$

7) $\dfrac{t^9}{5^1} = \dfrac{t^9}{5}$
8) $\dfrac{1}{k^{38}}$
9) v^{10}
10) $\dfrac{3^2}{r^{15}} = \dfrac{9}{r^{15}}$
11) w

12) c^{21}
13) $\dfrac{n^9}{4^3} = \dfrac{n^9}{64}$
14) $3^2 y^5 = 9y^5$
15) 1
16) $\dfrac{1}{5^3} = \dfrac{1}{125}$

17) $\dfrac{f^{17}}{6^2} = \dfrac{f^{17}}{36}$
18) $\dfrac{1}{s^7}$
19) $\dfrac{8^1}{q^2} = \dfrac{8}{q^2}$
20) $\dfrac{u^6}{4^2} = \dfrac{u^6}{16}$

1) $3^2 \cdot 5^2$
2) $x^4 \cdot y^4$
3) $4^{-p} \cdot 7^{-p}$
4) $a^x \cdot b^x$
5) $tooth^4 \cdot eye^4$
6) $6^{-d} \cdot 3^{-d}$
7) $2^3 \cdot 4^3 \cdot 5^3$
8) $\triangle^z \cdot \square^z$
9) $p^{-2} \cdot q^{-2}$
10) $c^y \cdot e^y$

1) $25y^2$
2) $8z^3$
3) $9a^2$
4) $64b^3$
5) $9n^2$
6) $-8d^3$

7) $36c^2$
8) $16h^2$
9) $125e^3$
10) $49f^2$
11) $64g^2$
12) $-8b^3$

13) $216p^3$
14) $8r^3$
15) $16t^2$
16) $81a^4$
17) $49k^2$
18) $-216m^3$

19) $16z^4$
20) $64j^3$
21) $27w^3$
22) $36x^2$
23) $343y^3$
24) $256p^4$

25) $-729n^3$
26) $27q^3$
27) $-64u^3$
28) $-512s^3$
29) $8v^3$
30) $1000x^3$

1) $\dfrac{1}{b}$

2) $\dfrac{ec^4}{7^2} = \dfrac{ec^4}{49}$

3) $\dfrac{1}{w^7}$

4) $\dfrac{q^5}{p}$

5) $\dfrac{n^6}{3^1} = \dfrac{n^6}{3}$

6) $\dfrac{3^2 z^8}{t^2} = \dfrac{9z^8}{t^2}$

7) $\dfrac{y^4}{9^2 x^{11}} = \dfrac{y^4}{81 x^{11}}$

8) $\dfrac{y^{12}}{k}$

9) $a^9 c^{11}$

10) $6^2 d^2 m^5 = 36 d^2 m^5$

1) $\dfrac{m^6}{n^6}$

2) $\dfrac{2^3}{5^3}$

3) $\dfrac{\triangle^x}{\square^x}$

4) $\dfrac{t^c}{w^c}$

5) $\dfrac{3^{-2}}{7^{-2}}$

6) $\dfrac{2^3}{9^3}$

7) $\dfrac{x^{-3}}{y^{-3}}$

8) $\dfrac{r^{-p}}{c^{-p}}$

9) $\dfrac{\bigstar^{\triangle}}{\square^{\triangle}}$

10) $\dfrac{3^{-4}}{10^{-4}}$

1) $\dfrac{r}{m^2}$

2) $\dfrac{1}{bc^5}$

3) $\dfrac{t^7}{3^2 w^7} = \dfrac{t^7}{9 w^7}$

4) $\dfrac{a^2}{c^2}$

5) $2^1 e^4 = 2e^4$

6) $\dfrac{v^3}{n^3}$

7) $\dfrac{5^3 r}{d^2} = \dfrac{125r}{d^2}$

8) $\dfrac{b^5}{c^8}$

9) $\dfrac{m^8 n^2}{7^2} = \dfrac{m^8 n^2}{49}$

10) $\dfrac{1}{2^3 \cdot 5^2} = \dfrac{1}{200}$

1) 4
2) 5
3) 2
4) 8
5) 7
6) 10
7) 9
8) 13
9) 11
10) 14

1) 25
2) 12a
3) $7mn^2$
4) w
5) 1/4
6) c
7) 19
8) 36xy
9) salami
10) $16p^2 q^2$

1) 18
2) m
3) rt
4) 1/8
5) ☺
6) q
7) $8w^2$
8) mnp
9) $100x^2 y$
10) magic

1) 169
2) y^2
3) 961
4) 225
5) r^4
6) 1/25
7) $144p^2$
8) 324
9) 12,321
10) $100x^2 y^2$

1) $-2\sqrt{8}$
2) $-6\sqrt{7}$
3) $10\sqrt{4} = 10 \cdot 2$
4) $13\sqrt{2}$
5) $-13\sqrt{12}$
6) $-9\sqrt{u}$
7) $9\sqrt{v}$
8) $-21\sqrt{a}$
9) $-16\sqrt{t}$
10) $17\sqrt{x}$

1) $\sqrt{10}$
2) $\sqrt{21}$
3) $\sqrt{ac}$
4) $\sqrt{dx}$
5) $\sqrt{6y}$
6) $\sqrt{13a}$
7) $\sqrt{frog \cdot toad}$
8) $\sqrt{rain \cdot cloud}$
9) $\sqrt{\text{☆} \cdot \square}$
10) $\sqrt{\triangle \cdot \text{☺}}$

1) 6
2) 4
3) 8
4) 12
5) 12
6) 14
7) a
8) m
9) 9x
10) 14y

11) 3x
12) 10c
13) 11e
14) 6k
15) 12p
16) 7w
17) 9z
18) 10u
19) 8n
20) 14r

1) $\sqrt{8} \cdot \sqrt{5}$
2) $\sqrt{11} \cdot \sqrt{7}$
3) $\sqrt{m} \cdot \sqrt{p}$
4) $\sqrt{x} \cdot \sqrt{y}$
5) $\sqrt{15} \cdot \sqrt{r}$
6) $\sqrt{c^2} \cdot \sqrt{16} = 4c$
7) $\sqrt{red} \cdot \sqrt{blue}$
8) $\sqrt{foot} \cdot \sqrt{hand}$
9) $\sqrt{\text{☆}} \cdot \sqrt{\text{◉}}$
10) $\sqrt{\text{⊗}} \cdot \sqrt{\triangle}$

1) $2\sqrt{2}$
2) $2\sqrt{3}$
3) $3\sqrt{2}$
4) $2\sqrt{5}$
5) $4\sqrt{2}$
6) $3\sqrt{5}$
7) $5\sqrt{2}$
8) $2\sqrt{13}$
9) $2\sqrt{15}$
10) $3\sqrt{7}$

11) $6\sqrt{2}$
12) $5\sqrt{3}$
13) $4\sqrt{5}$
14) $3\sqrt{10}$
15) $4\sqrt{6}$
16) $7\sqrt{2}$
17) $8\sqrt{2}$
18) $3\sqrt{15}$
19) $2\sqrt{34}$
20) $10\sqrt{2}$

21) 12b
22) 9ms
23) 8q
24) 11a
25) 6x
26) 3yk
27) 13w
28) 10ef
29) 14nt
30) 7r

31) $4w\sqrt{2}$
32) $2g\sqrt{3}$
33) $4v\sqrt{5}$
34) $3rp\sqrt{5}$
35) $5kg\sqrt{3}$
36) $3b\sqrt{7c}$
37) $3y\sqrt{2x}$
38) $4\sqrt{6u}$
39) $8\sqrt{r}$
40) 9s

41) $ab\sqrt{x}$
42) $p\sqrt{m}$
43) $6y\sqrt{x}$
44) $wd\sqrt{t}$
45) $9bc\sqrt{a}$
46) $2wz\sqrt{2}$
47) $2em\sqrt{5}$
48) $5pr\sqrt{3q}$
49) 8ta
50) $6ns\sqrt{6tv}$

1) True
2) False
3) False
4) True
5) False
6) False
7) True
8) True
9) False
10) True

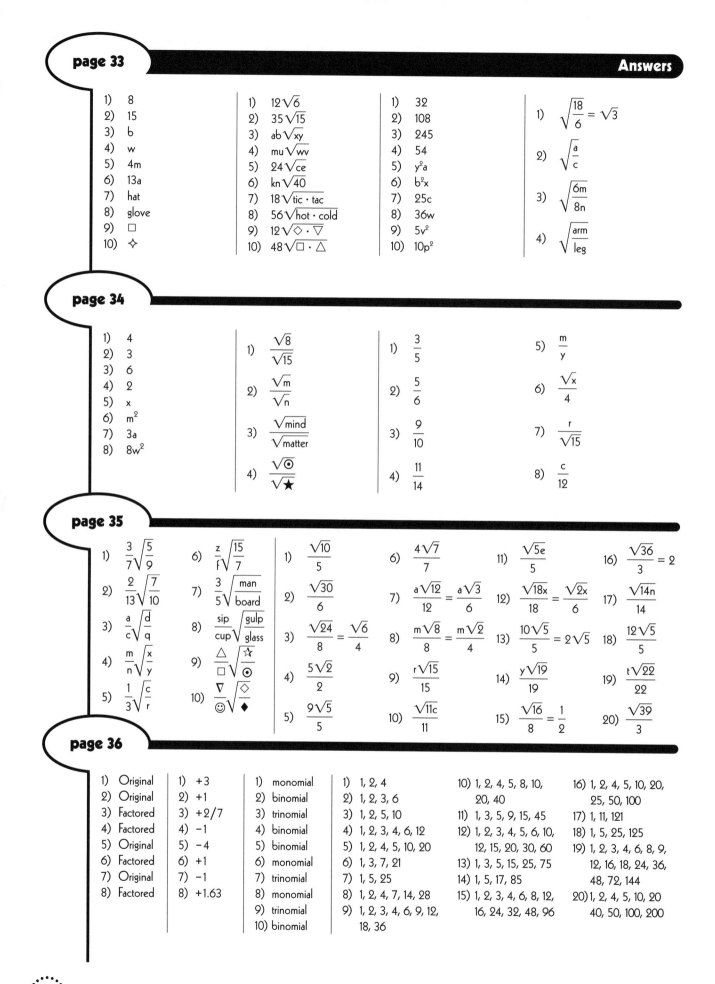

page 33

1) 8
2) 15
3) b
4) w
5) 4m
6) 13a
7) hat
8) glove
9) □
10) ✧

1) $12\sqrt{6}$
2) $35\sqrt{15}$
3) $ab\sqrt{xy}$
4) $mu\sqrt{wv}$
5) $24\sqrt{ce}$
6) $kn\sqrt{40}$
7) $18\sqrt{tic \cdot tac}$
8) $56\sqrt{hot \cdot cold}$
9) $12\sqrt{\diamond \cdot \triangledown}$
10) $48\sqrt{\square \cdot \triangle}$

1) 32
2) 108
3) 245
4) 54
5) y^2a
6) b^2x
7) $25c$
8) $36w$
9) $5v^2$
10) $10p^2$

1) $\sqrt{\dfrac{18}{6}} = \sqrt{3}$
2) $\sqrt{\dfrac{a}{c}}$
3) $\sqrt{\dfrac{6m}{8n}}$
4) $\sqrt{\dfrac{arm}{leg}}$

page 34

1) 4
2) 3
3) 6
4) 2
5) x
6) m^2
7) 3a
8) $8w^2$

1) $\dfrac{\sqrt{8}}{\sqrt{15}}$
2) $\dfrac{\sqrt{m}}{\sqrt{n}}$
3) $\dfrac{\sqrt{mind}}{\sqrt{matter}}$
4) $\dfrac{\sqrt{\odot}}{\sqrt{\star}}$

1) $\dfrac{3}{5}$
2) $\dfrac{5}{6}$
3) $\dfrac{9}{10}$
4) $\dfrac{11}{14}$

5) $\dfrac{m}{y}$
6) $\dfrac{\sqrt{x}}{4}$
7) $\dfrac{r}{\sqrt{15}}$
8) $\dfrac{c}{12}$

page 35

1) $\dfrac{3}{7}\sqrt{\dfrac{5}{9}}$
2) $\dfrac{2}{13}\sqrt{\dfrac{7}{10}}$
3) $\dfrac{a}{c}\sqrt{\dfrac{d}{q}}$
4) $\dfrac{m}{n}\sqrt{\dfrac{x}{y}}$
5) $\dfrac{1}{3}\sqrt{\dfrac{c}{r}}$

6) $\dfrac{z}{f}\sqrt{\dfrac{15}{7}}$
7) $\dfrac{3}{5}\sqrt{\dfrac{man}{board}}$
8) $\dfrac{sip}{cup}\sqrt{\dfrac{gulp}{glass}}$
9) $\dfrac{\triangle}{\square}\sqrt{\dfrac{\star}{\odot}}$
10) $\dfrac{\triangledown}{\copyright}\sqrt{\dfrac{\diamond}{\blacklozenge}}$

1) $\dfrac{\sqrt{10}}{5}$
2) $\dfrac{\sqrt{30}}{6}$
3) $\dfrac{\sqrt{24}}{8} = \dfrac{\sqrt{6}}{4}$
4) $\dfrac{5\sqrt{2}}{2}$
5) $\dfrac{9\sqrt{5}}{5}$

6) $\dfrac{4\sqrt{7}}{7}$
7) $\dfrac{a\sqrt{12}}{12} = \dfrac{a\sqrt{3}}{6}$
8) $\dfrac{m\sqrt{8}}{8} = \dfrac{m\sqrt{2}}{4}$
9) $\dfrac{r\sqrt{15}}{15}$
10) $\dfrac{\sqrt{11c}}{11}$

11) $\dfrac{\sqrt{5e}}{5}$
12) $\dfrac{\sqrt{18x}}{18} = \dfrac{\sqrt{2x}}{6}$
13) $\dfrac{10\sqrt{5}}{5} = 2\sqrt{5}$
14) $\dfrac{y\sqrt{19}}{19}$
15) $\dfrac{\sqrt{16}}{8} = \dfrac{1}{2}$

16) $\dfrac{\sqrt{36}}{3} = 2$
17) $\dfrac{\sqrt{14n}}{14}$
18) $\dfrac{12\sqrt{5}}{5}$
19) $\dfrac{t\sqrt{22}}{22}$
20) $\dfrac{\sqrt{39}}{3}$

page 36

1) Original
2) Original
3) Factored
4) Factored
5) Original
6) Factored
7) Original
8) Factored

1) +3
2) +1
3) +2/7
4) −1
5) −4
6) +1
7) −1
8) +1.63

1) monomial
2) binomial
3) trinomial
4) binomial
5) binomial
6) monomial
7) trinomial
8) monomial
9) trinomial
10) binomial

1) 1, 2, 4
2) 1, 2, 3, 6
3) 1, 2, 5, 10
4) 1, 2, 3, 4, 6, 12
5) 1, 2, 4, 5, 10, 20
6) 1, 3, 7, 21
7) 1, 5, 25
8) 1, 2, 4, 7, 14, 28
9) 1, 2, 3, 4, 6, 9, 12, 18, 36

10) 1, 2, 4, 5, 8, 10, 20, 40
11) 1, 3, 5, 9, 15, 45
12) 1, 2, 3, 4, 5, 6, 10, 12, 15, 20, 30, 60
13) 1, 3, 5, 15, 25, 75
14) 1, 5, 17, 85
15) 1, 2, 3, 4, 6, 8, 12, 16, 24, 32, 48, 96

16) 1, 2, 4, 5, 10, 20, 25, 50, 100
17) 1, 11, 121
18) 1, 5, 25, 125
19) 1, 2, 3, 4, 6, 8, 9, 12, 16, 18, 24, 36, 48, 72, 144
20) 1, 2, 4, 5, 10, 20, 40, 50, 100, 200

1) 1, 2, 3, 4, 6, 12, p, p^2
2) 1, 2, 4, 8, x, y, z, xy, xz, yz, xyz
3) 1, 3, 5, 15, b, c, b^2, bc, b^2c
4) 1, 13, w, v, w^2, v^2, w^2v, wv^2, wv, w^2v^2
5) 1, 2, 4, 8, 16, p, q, q^2, pq, pq^2

1) 7
2) 3
3) 14
4) 12
5) 18
6) 8
7) 27
8) 10
9) 20
10) 23

1) 3m
2) 5
3) 4b
4) y
5) 14c
6) $6p^2$
7) ax
8) 6
9) 10xy
10) $8b^2c^2$

11) $7x^2yz$
12) $6ab^2$
13) 2
14) 1
15) $9k^2$

1) 4m(3m + 1)
2) $5k^2$(3k – 2)
3) 7x(1 – 4x)
4) 6(3 + w^3)
5) $6x^2$(4 + 3x)
6) 8ac(2a – 3c)
7) 6np($3m^2$ + 5p)
8) $2v^2$(3ru – 2mp)
9) 7wxy(2w – 3)
10) 4abc(abc + 2)

11) 4($3d^2$ – 2d – 1)
12) 5r($3r^2$ + r – 2)
13) 6x(y^2 – 3y – 2)
14) 14ab(a + 2b + 3)
15) x^2(5 – 7x + $12x^2$)
16) $3mnp^2$(2m – 5n + 3p)
17) $9r^2t$($9t^2$ – 7t + 4)
18) $27u^3$($3v^4$ + v^3 – 2)
19) $2c^2e$(3 – 4e – 6c)
20) $4p^2q^2$(9q + 11pq + 7)

1) No
2) No
3) Yes
4) No
5) Yes
6) No
7) No
8) Yes
9) Yes
10) No

11) Yes
12) No
13) No
14) Yes
15) Yes
16) No
17) Yes
18) No
19) Yes
20) Yes

1) (+1, +4), (–1, –4), (+2, +2), (–2, –2)
2) (+1, –4), (–1, +4), (+2, –2)
3) (+1, +6), (–1, –6), (+2, +3), (–2, –3)
4) (+1, –6), (–1, +6), (+2, –3), (–2, +3)
5) (+1, +8), (–1, –8), (+2, +4), (–2, –4)
6) (+1, –8), (–1, +8), (+2, –4), (–2, +4)
7) (+1, +14), (–1, –14), (+2, +7), (–2, –7)
8) (+1, –14), (–1, +14), (+2, –7), (–2, +7)
9) (+1, +24), (–1, –24), (+2, +12), (–2, –12), (+3, +8), (–3, –8), (+4, +6), (–4, –6)
10) (+1, –24), (–1, +24), (+2, –12), (–2, +12), (+3, –8), (–3, +8), (+4, –6), (–4, +6)
11) (+1, +27), (–1, –27), (+3, +9), (–3, –9)
12) (+1, –27), (–1, +27), (+3, –9), (–3, +9)
13) (+1, +30), (–1, –30), (+2, +15), (–2, –15), (+3, +10), (–3, –10), (+5, +6), (–5, –6)
14) (+1, –30), (–1, +30), (+2, –15), (–2, +15), (+3, –10), (–3, +10), (+5, –6), (–5, +6)
15) (+1, +48), (–1, –48), (+2, +24), (–2, –24), (+3, +16), (–3, –16), (+4, +12), (–4, –12), (+6, +8), (–6, –8)

1) (+2, +2)
2) (–4, +1)
3) (–6, –1)
4) (+3, –2)
5) (–4, –2)
6) (–8, +1)
7) (+7, +2)
8) (–14, +1)
9) (+12, +2)
10) (+8, –3)
11) (+9, +3)
12) (–9, +3)
13) (–5, –6)
14) (+10, –3)
15) (+8, +6)

Answers

page 40

1) $(c + 1)(c + 3)$
2) $(m + 2)(m + 3)$
3) $(w + 2)(w + 4)$
4) $(x + 1)(x + 6)$
5) $(e + 2)(e + 5)$
6) $(m + 3)(m + 4)$
7) $(t + 1)(t + 7)$
8) $(u + 3)(u + 6)$
9) $(y + 4)(y + 5)$
10) $(x + 1)(x + 9)$
11) $(a + 3)(a + 7)$
12) $(b + 2)(b + 9)$
13) $(p + 3)(p + 8)$
14) $(m + 4)(m + 7)$
15) $(r + 5)(r + 6)$
16) $(p + 3)(p + 9)$
17) $(x + 4)(x + 8)$
18) $(m + 2)(m + 11)$
19) $(q + 3)(q + 10)$
20) $(c + 4)(c + 9)$
21) $(e + 5)(e + 8)$
22) $(r + 6)(r + 7)$
23) $(x + 5)(x + 9)$
24) $(b + 6)(b + 8)$
25) $(n + 7)(n + 8)$
26) $(p + 4)(p + 12)$
27) $(s + 6)(s + 10)$
28) $(x + 5)(x + 12)$
29) $(k + 6)(k + 12)$
30) $(c + 5)(c + 15)$

1) $(x - 1)(x - 3)$
2) $(b - 2)(b - 2)$
3) $(z - 1)(z - 4)$
4) $(u - 2)(u - 3)$
5) $(y - 1)(y - 5)$
6) $(w - 2)(w - 4)$
7) $(b - 1)(b - 6)$
8) $(k - 2)(k - 5)$
9) $(d - 3)(d - 4)$
10) $(w - 3)(w - 10)$
11) $(x - 4)(x - 9)$
12) $(m - 2)(m - 30)$
13) $(e - 3)(e - 20)$
14) $(g - 5)(g - 12)$
15) $(f - 6)(f - 10)$
16) $(k - 3)(k - 32)$
17) $(s - 4)(s - 24)$
18) $(n - 6)(n - 16)$
19) $(p - 8)(p - 12)$
20) $(x - 4)(x - 25)$
21) $(t - 3)(t - 9)$
22) $(u - 5)(u - 7)$
23) $(q - 3)(q - 12)$
24) $(v - 5)(v - 10)$
25) $(z - 7)(z - 8)$
26) $(r - 3)(r - 15)$
27) $(y - 6)(y - 12)$
28) $(a - 8)(a - 10)$
29) $(c - 6)(c - 15)$
30) $(d - 10)(d - 11)$

page 41

1) $(m + 9)(m - 3)$
2) $(b + 10)(b - 4)$
3) $(a + 11)(a - 5)$
4) $(z + 6)(z - 3)$
5) $(y + 7)(y - 4)$
6) $(c + 8)(c - 5)$
7) $(r + 9)(r - 6)$
8) $(f + 4)(f - 3)$
9) $(p + 5)(p - 4)$
10) $(x + 14)(x - 2)$
11) $(d + 7)(d - 4)$
12) $(w + 20)(w - 2)$
13) $(b + 40)(b - 1)$
14) $(e + 21)(e - 2)$
15) $(k + 15)(k - 3)$
16) $(v + 9)(v - 5)$
17) $(g + 48)(g - 3)$
18) $(f + 36)(f - 4)$
19) $(k + 24)(k - 6)$
20) $(u + 18)(u - 8)$
21) $(m + 13)(m - 3)$
22) $(t + 16)(t - 6)$
23) $(p + 20)(p - 10)$
24) $(m + 14)(m - 2)$
25) $(n + 16)(n - 4)$
26) $(d + 18)(d - 6)$
27) $(q + 20)(q - 8)$
28) $(c + 16)(c - 1)$
29) $(r + 22)(r - 7)$
30) $(s + 25)(s - 10)$

1) $(k + 2)(k - 7)$
2) $(h + 3)(h - 8)$
3) $(m + 5)(m - 10)$
4) $(x + 6)(x - 14)$
5) $(y + 8)(y - 16)$
6) $(z + 3)(z - 11)$
7) $(a + 2)(a - 13)$
8) $(n + 4)(n - 15)$
9) $(b + 3)(b - 15)$
10) $(z + 2)(z - 14)$
11) $(p + 3)(p - 12)$
12) $(m + 4)(m - 9)$
13) $(f + 2)(f - 18)$
14) $(q + 3)(q - 10)$
15) $(c + 2)(c - 15)$
16) $(e + 5)(e - 6)$
17) $(d + 1)(d - 21)$
18) $(r + 3)(r - 7)$
19) $(c + 5)(c - 17)$
20) $(d + 1)(d - 85)$
21) $(s + 1)(s - 15)$
22) $(b + 3)(b - 17)$
23) $(e + 6)(e - 20)$
24) $(t + 2)(t - 19)$
25) $(a + 5)(a - 22)$
26) $(f + 4)(f - 28)$
27) $(u + 8)(u - 14)$
28) $(g + 2)(g - 56)$
29) $(v + 1)(v - 125)$
30) $(w + 5)(w - 25)$

page 42

1) $+x$ and $+x$
2) $+x$ and -3
3) $+5$ and $+x$
4) $+5$ and -3
5) $+a$ and $+a$
6) $+a$ and $+6$
7) -2 and $+a$
8) -2 and $+6$

1) $k^2 + 5k + 6$
2) $m^2 + 6m + 5$
3) $v^2 + 10v + 24$
4) $d^2 + 5d - 24$
5) $u^2 + 12u + 27$
6) $t^2 - 4t - 45$
7) $e^2 - 8e - 20$
8) $w^2 + 7w + 6$
9) $f^2 - f - 72$
10) $x^2 - 14x + 33$
11) $g^2 - 21g + 90$
12) $c^2 + 16c - 57$
13) $s^2 - 24s + 140$
14) $b^2 + 7b - 78$
15) $n^2 - 26n + 144$
16) $x^2 - 10x - 75$
17) $c^2 + 4c - 117$
18) $t^2 + 19t + 48$
19) $r^2 - 24r + 143$
20) $d^2 - 14d - 95$
21) $h^2 + 7h - 98$
22) $k^2 + 30k + 216$
23) $v^2 - 23v + 42$
24) $u^2 - u - 182$
25) $z^2 + 3z - 88$
26) $p^2 - 25p + 144$
27) $a^2 + 7a - 120$
28) $q^2 + 6q - 187$
29) $r^2 - 25r + 156$
30) $y^2 - 37y + 340$

1) $(x + 5)(x - 5)$
2) $(m + 7)(m - 7)$
3) $(k + 10)(k - 10)$
4) $(w + 12)(w - 12)$
5) $(2c + 6)(2c - 6)$
6) $(3w + 8)(3w - 8)$
7) $(5y + 5)(5y - 5)$
8) $(4c + 2)(4c - 2)$
9) $(6n + 1)(6n - 1)$
10) $(2p + 3r)(2p - 3r)$
11) $(3xy + 4z)(3xy - 4z)$
12) $(a + b)(a - b)$
13) $(np + 2v)(np - 2v)$
14) $(5 + x)(5 - x)$
15) $(9 + 1)(9 - 1)$

Answers

page 43

1) m
2) 1/p
3) 1/xy
4) a

5) r
6) ce
7) 1/k
8) $1/p^2$

1) a
2) 3 and y
3) (m + n)
4) x
5) x and y

6) m
7) e
8) (s + t)
9) c
10) v and n

1) b
2) 5
3) 3
4) $\dfrac{p}{q} + 1$

5) 9 – d
6) y
7) $\dfrac{b + c}{3}$

8) $\dfrac{u}{v} + 1$
9) 7x – 1
10) rm

page 44

1) x + 2y
2) b + c
3) $\dfrac{3m + 5n}{2}$
4) $\dfrac{2}{u - 3v}$
5) 2s – 5t
6) $\dfrac{1}{e + v}$

7) $\dfrac{2w}{x + 3y}$
8) 3d – 2e + 5f
9) $\dfrac{p - 3q}{2}$
10) $\dfrac{5n + 2r - 6k}{3}$

1) $\dfrac{m + n}{2(b + c)}$
2) $\dfrac{1 - 2y}{2 - 3y}$
3) $\dfrac{d + 3f}{2d - 3f}$
4) $\dfrac{2(3n - r)}{3n + 2r}$
5) $\dfrac{4 + 5e}{3(2 + 3e)}$

6) $\dfrac{2 - 3m}{2(m + 4)}$
7) $\dfrac{2(a - 2c)}{2a - 3c}$
8) $\dfrac{rv - 2sq}{3xy + 4wz}$
9) $\dfrac{2(nr + 2st)}{3ns + 5rt}$
10) $\dfrac{2x + 3z}{3z - 4x}$

page 45

1) $\dfrac{3(g^2 - 2)}{g(g + 1)}$
2) $\dfrac{3y - 2}{y(2y + 5)}$
3) $\dfrac{2c(1 + 2c^2)}{4c^2 - 1}$
4) $\dfrac{2n + 3}{2n(n^2 + 1)}$
5) $\dfrac{2(3 - 4r)}{5(1 + 3r^2)}$

6) 2a + 6
7) $t^2 - 3t$
8) $3u - 4u^2$
9) 2z – 3
10) $2c^2 - 3d$

1) Yes
2) No
3) No
4) Yes
5) No
6) No
7) Yes
8) Yes
9) No
10) Yes

1) num.: 5, (d + g)
   denom.: 3, 5, 15, (d + g)
2) num.: n, (r + t)
   denom.: (r + t)
3) num.: 3, 9, (e + f)
   denom.: 2, 3, 4, 6, 12, e
4) num.: (n + p – r)
   denom.: r, (n + p)
5) num.: (s – t + v)
   denom.: (t + v)

6) num.: (x – y)
   denom.: w, (x – y)
7) num.: 2, 3, 6, m, m^2
   denom.: (u + m)
8) num.: 2, 4, (p – q)
   denom.: 2, 3, 6, (p + q)
9) num.: 3, (b + c)
   denom.: (b + c), $(b + c)^2$
10) num.: x, x^2, (y – z)
    denom.: (y – z), (y + z), $(y^2 - z^2)$

page 46

1) 1/2
2) 3/5
3) 1
4) 1/3
5) 3u/2w
6) 9
7) 1/6
8) x/y
9) 3/7u
10) $2c/d^2$

1) $\dfrac{x}{z} + \dfrac{y}{z}$
2) $\dfrac{a}{c} + \dfrac{b}{c} - \dfrac{3}{c}$
3) $\dfrac{n^2}{r} - \dfrac{r}{r}$
4) $\dfrac{ant}{spider} - \dfrac{mouse}{spider}$
5) $\dfrac{11}{21} - \dfrac{t}{21}$

6) $\dfrac{p}{z} + \dfrac{2}{z}$
7) $\dfrac{\bullet}{\bigstar} + \dfrac{\odot}{\bigstar}$
8) $\dfrac{c}{2} + \dfrac{d}{2}$
9) $\dfrac{3v}{2x} + \dfrac{2u}{2x} - \dfrac{4x}{2x}$
10) $\dfrac{k^2}{4} - \dfrac{4k}{4}$

1) $\dfrac{4}{d} + 1$
2) $1 + \dfrac{e}{c}$
3) $\dfrac{1}{x} - \dfrac{y}{x^2}$
4) $\dfrac{p^2}{q} - 1$
5) $\dfrac{a}{b^2} + 1$

6) $\dfrac{n}{r} - r$
7) $1 + \dfrac{k}{v} + \dfrac{w}{v}$
8) $\dfrac{u}{s} + \dfrac{t}{s} + 1$
9) $1 - \dfrac{y^2}{x^2}$
10) $1 + \dfrac{b}{a} - \dfrac{c}{a}$

1) Left side
2) Number term
3) Variable term
4) Right side
5) Variable
6) Number term
7) Left side
8) Variable term
9) Variable
10) Right side

1) $5a - 8 = 3a - 2$
2) $4k - 16 = 8k + 8$
3) $3p + 15 = 60 - 2p$
4) $7b + 17 = 4b + 32$
5) $28 - 5e = 40 - 6e$
6) $5m + 20 = 2m + 8$
7) $6q - 22 = 8q + 6$
8) $c + 15 = 6c - 20$
9) $3f = 6f + 15$
10) $7n - 26 = 3n + 6$

11) $9d - 11 = 6d - 5$
12) $5r + 11 = 2r - 19$
13) $12s + 14 = 6s + 20$
14) $30v - 100 = 26v$
15) $10y - 26 = 8y - 6$
16) $25 - t = 10$
17) $7w + 33 = 5w + 19$
18) $4z - 15 = -8z - 27$
19) $u + 21 = 4u + 60$
20) $-24x - 12 = 42 - 33x$

1) $x = 5$
2) $b = 8$
3) $r = -3$
4) $v = -7$
5) $n = 7$
6) $d = -5$
7) $k = 18$
8) $t = 15$
9) $e = 6$
10) $q = -4$
11) $m = -6$
12) $w = 7$
13) $y = 35$
14) $f = 12$
15) $c = -60$
16) $s = -48$
17) $a = +6$
18) $p = +11$
19) $u = +2$
20) $z = 3$

1) $2a = 6$
2) $3d = 6$
3) $4k = -24$
4) $5p = 45$
5) $3b = 15$
6) $e = 12$
7) $3m = -12$
8) $2q = -28$
9) $5c = 35$
10) $3f = -15$
11) $4n = 32$
12) $3r = -30$
13) $6s = 6$
14) $4v = 100$
15) $2y = 20$
16) $t = 15$
17) $2w = -14$
18) $12z = -12$
19) $3u = -39$
20) $9x = 54$

1) $a = 3$
2) $d = 2$
3) $k = -6$
4) $p = 9$
5) $b = 5$
6) $e = 12$
7) $m = -4$
8) $q = -14$
9) $c = 7$
10) $f = -5$
11) $n = 8$
12) $r = -10$
13) $s = 1$
14) $v = 25$
15) $y = 10$
16) $t = 15$
17) $w = -7$
18) $z = -1$
19) $u = -13$
20) $x = 6$

1) $a = 5$
2) $e = 12$
3) $r = -1$
4) $n = 13$
5) $b = -10$
6) $f = 4$
7) $k = 10$
8) $p = -5$
9) $c = 7$
10) $d = 8$
11) $m = -6$
12) $q = -5$
13) $v = -11$
14) $z = -12$
15) $u = 15$
16) $s = -9$
17) $w = 2$
18) $x = -20$
19) $y = 6$
20) $t = -17$

1) q = 20
2) r = 8
3) v = 19
4) a = 6
5) p = −5
6) n = 15
7) b = −14
8) t = 9
9) u = 12
10) c = −4
11) e = 2
12) m = 7
13) x = −12
14) d = −8
15) y = 10

1) n = 3
2) a = 4
3) g = 10
4) p = 7
5) b = 5
6) r = 9
7) z = 15
8) x = 6
9) s = 12
10) c = 14
11) v = 8
12) d = 11
13) t = 7
14) e = 10
15) u = 15

1) m = +5 or
   m = −5
2) n = +8 or
   n = −8
3) 3r − 4 = +13 or
   3r − 4 = −13
4) 10 − y = +1 or
   10 − y = −1

1) a = +6 or a = −3
2) k = −3 or k = +11/3
3) n = −1 or n = −4
4) b = +2 or b = −4
5) r = +1 or r = −4
6) e = +2 or e = +6
7) c = +1 or c = −1/4
8) t = −1 or t = +5
9) d = +8 or d = −4
10) p = +5 or p = −3/5

1) v = −4 or v = −2
2) m = −2 or m = 6
3) u = 3 or u = 7
4) t = −8 or t = 4
5) s = −3 or s = −5
6) x = −5 or x = 9
7) k = 4 or k = 5
8) c = −12 or c = 7
9) r = −6 or r = −1
10) y = −2 or y = 11

11) w = 6 or w = 9
12) p = −7 or p = 1
13) z = −8 or z = −4
14) q = −10 or q = 2
15) n = −5 or n = 15

1) $\sqrt{40} \approx 6.3$ cm.
2) $\sqrt{116} \approx 10.8$ inches
3) $\sqrt{169} = 13$ miles
4) $\sqrt{625} = 25$ feet
5) $\sqrt{306} \approx 17.5$ meters
6) $\sqrt{373} \approx 19.3$ inches
7) $\sqrt{466} \approx 21.6$ feet
8) $\sqrt{681} = 41$ yards
9) $\sqrt{3721} = 61$ lightyears
10) $\sqrt{629} \approx 25.1$ mm.

1) $\sqrt{5} \approx 2.2$ yards
2) $\sqrt{9} = 3$ meters
3) $\sqrt{144} = 12$ feet
4) $\sqrt{45} \approx 6.7$ cm.
5) $\sqrt{189} \approx 13.7$ mm.
6) $\sqrt{576} = 24$ inches
7) $\sqrt{64} = 8$ feet
8) $\sqrt{1600} = 40$ miles
9) $\sqrt{112} \approx 10.6$ yards
10) $\sqrt{32} \approx 5.7$ meters

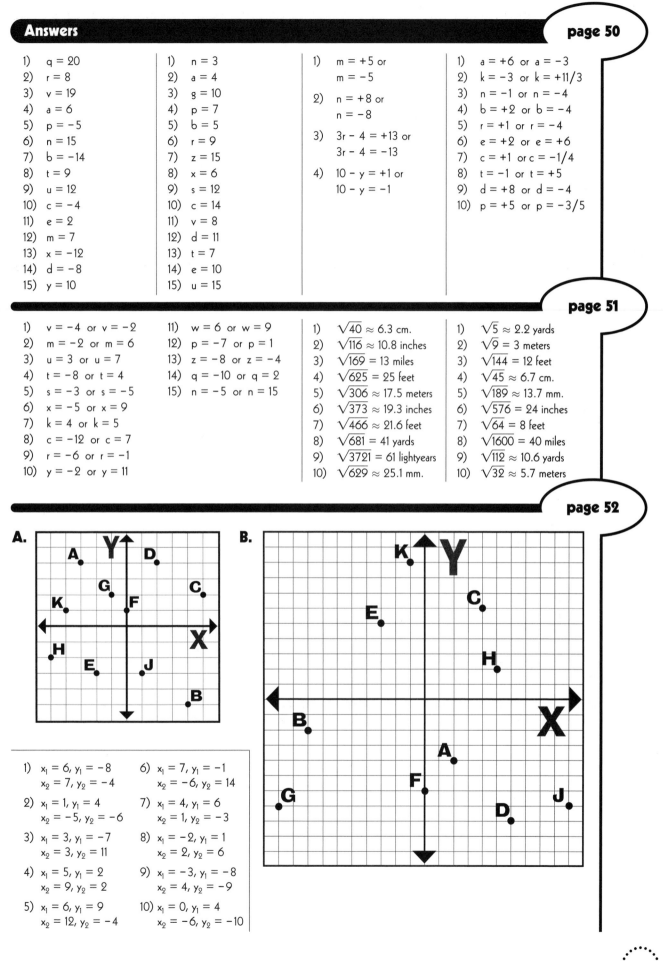

A.

B.

1) $x_1 = 6, y_1 = −8$
   $x_2 = 7, y_2 = −4$
2) $x_1 = 1, y_1 = 4$
   $x_2 = −5, y_2 = −6$
3) $x_1 = 3, y_1 = −7$
   $x_2 = 3, y_2 = 11$
4) $x_1 = 5, y_1 = 2$
   $x_2 = 9, y_2 = 2$
5) $x_1 = 6, y_1 = 9$
   $x_2 = 12, y_2 = −4$

6) $x_1 = 7, y_1 = −1$
   $x_2 = −6, y_2 = 14$
7) $x_1 = 4, y_1 = 6$
   $x_2 = 1, y_2 = −3$
8) $x_1 = −2, y_1 = 1$
   $x_2 = 2, y_2 = 6$
9) $x_1 = −3, y_1 = −8$
   $x_2 = 4, y_2 = −9$
10) $x_1 = 0, y_1 = 4$
    $x_2 = −6, y_2 = −10$

1) m = 1/2   3) m = 1/4   5) m = −1   7) m = 3   9) m = −10
2) m = −1   4) m = 2   6) m = 4   8) m = −2/5   10) m = 1

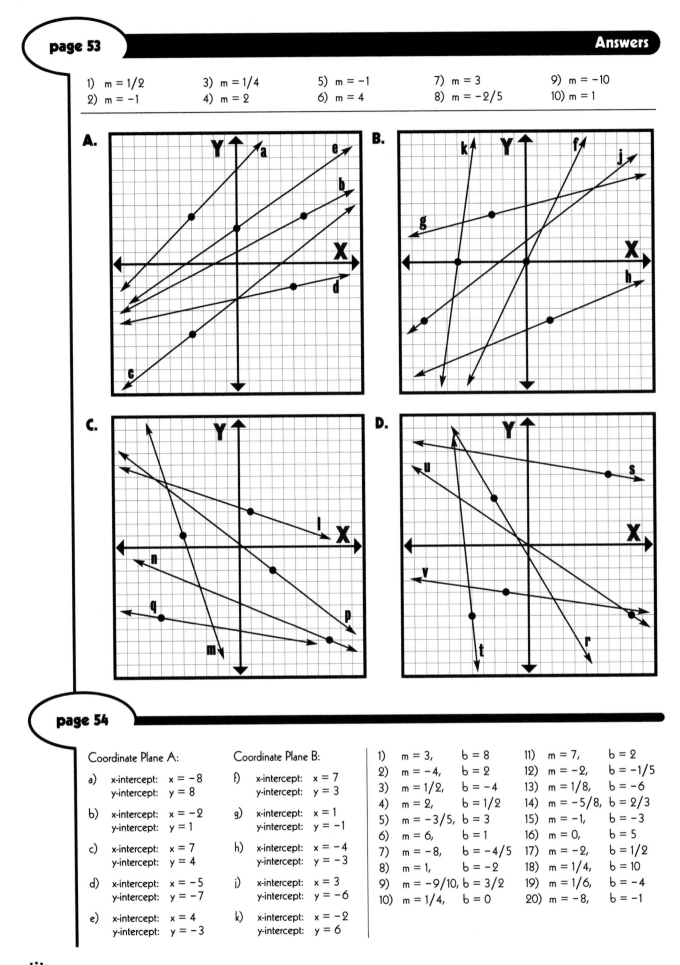

Coordinate Plane A:

a) x-intercept: x = −8
    y-intercept: y = 8

b) x-intercept: x = −2
    y-intercept: y = 1

c) x-intercept: x = 7
    y-intercept: y = 4

d) x-intercept: x = −5
    y-intercept: y = −7

e) x-intercept: x = 4
    y-intercept: y = −3

Coordinate Plane B:

f) x-intercept: x = 7
    y-intercept: y = 3

g) x-intercept: x = 1
    y-intercept: y = −1

h) x-intercept: x = −4
    y-intercept: y = −3

j) x-intercept: x = 3
    y-intercept: y = −6

k) x-intercept: x = −2
    y-intercept: y = 6

1) m = 3,   b = 8
2) m = −4,   b = 2
3) m = 1/2,   b = −4
4) m = 2,   b = 1/2
5) m = −3/5,   b = 3
6) m = 6,   b = 1
7) m = −8,   b = −4/5
8) m = 1,   b = −2
9) m = −9/10,   b = 3/2
10) m = 1/4,   b = 0

11) m = 7,   b = 2
12) m = −2,   b = −1/5
13) m = 1/8,   b = −6
14) m = −5/8,   b = 2/3
15) m = −1,   b = −3
16) m = 0,   b = 5
17) m = −2,   b = 1/2
18) m = 1/4,   b = 10
19) m = 1/6,   b = −4
20) m = −8,   b = −1

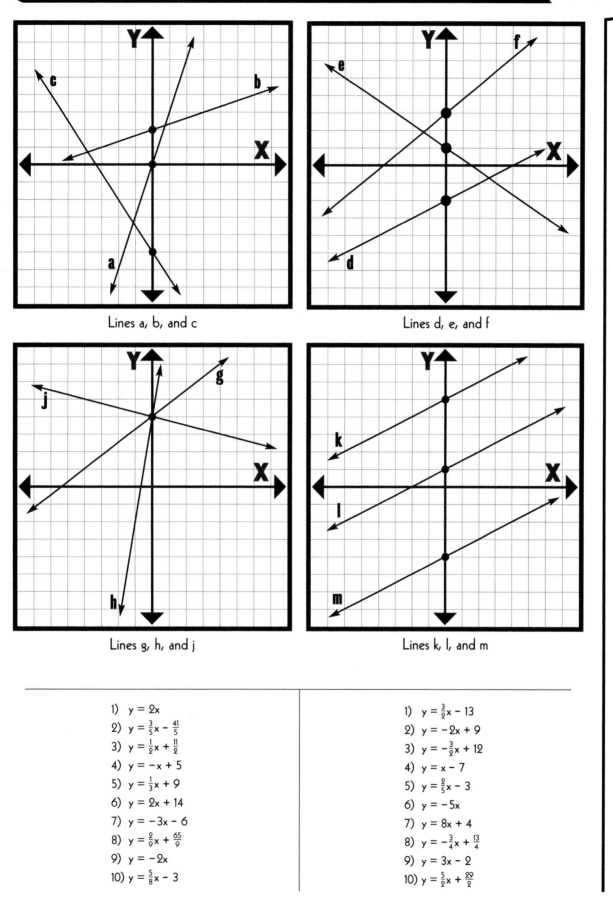

Lines a, b, and c

Lines d, e, and f

Lines g, h, and j

Lines k, l, and m

1) $y = 2x$

2) $y = \frac{3}{5}x - \frac{41}{5}$

3) $y = \frac{1}{2}x + \frac{11}{2}$

4) $y = -x + 5$

5) $y = \frac{1}{3}x + 9$

6) $y = 2x + 14$

7) $y = -3x - 6$

8) $y = \frac{2}{9}x + \frac{65}{9}$

9) $y = -2x$

10) $y = \frac{5}{8}x - 3$

1) $y = \frac{3}{2}x - 13$

2) $y = -2x + 9$

3) $y = -\frac{3}{2}x + 12$

4) $y = x - 7$

5) $y = \frac{2}{5}x - 3$

6) $y = -5x$

7) $y = 8x + 4$

8) $y = -\frac{3}{4}x + \frac{13}{4}$

9) $y = 3x - 2$

10) $y = \frac{5}{2}x + \frac{29}{2}$

Answers

1) $y = 2x + 6$
2) $y = 3x - 8$
3) $y = -3x + 2$
4) $y = x - 2$
5) $y = -2x + \frac{4}{3}$
6) $y = -\frac{1}{2}x + 2$
7) $y = -\frac{5}{7}x + \frac{5}{7}$
8) $y = 6x - 10$
9) $y = \frac{8}{3}x - 4$
10) $y = \frac{3}{2}x + 6$

11) $y = 3x - \frac{21}{5}$
12) $y = -x + 3$
13) $y = \frac{8}{5}x - 2$
14) $y = \frac{1}{3}x - \frac{1}{3}$
15) $y = -\frac{14}{3}x - 5$
16) $y = -\frac{1}{3}x + 3$
17) $y = 2x - 4$
18) $y = \frac{3}{5}x + 1$
19) $y = \frac{5}{6}x - \frac{8}{3}$
20) $y = -x - \frac{14}{3}$

A.

a) $x = 4$ b) $y = 2$
c) $x = -6$ d) $y = -3$

B.

e) $y = 3$ f) $x = 2$
g) $y = -2$ h) $x = -3$

1) $(-2, 5)$
2) $(9, 2)$
3) $(-1, -2)$
4) $(3, -5)$
5) $(1, -6)$
6) $(8, 22)$
7) $(3, 0)$
8) $(12, 1)$
9) $(-2, -10)$
10) $(0, 2)$

11) $(2, -2)$
12) $(2, 6)$
13) $(-3, 3)$
14) $(-10, 5)$
15) $(-3, -2)$
16) $(0, 8)$
17) $(-2, -9)$
18) $(5, -3)$
19) $(3, 10)$
20) $(2, 5)$

1) $(-2, 3)$

2) $(1, 0)$

3) $(-1, 0)$

4) $(3, 3)$

5) $(2, -1)$

6) $(-2, -4)$

7) $(5, 5)$

8) $(-2, 5)$

9) $(0, 2)$

10) $(-1, 3)$

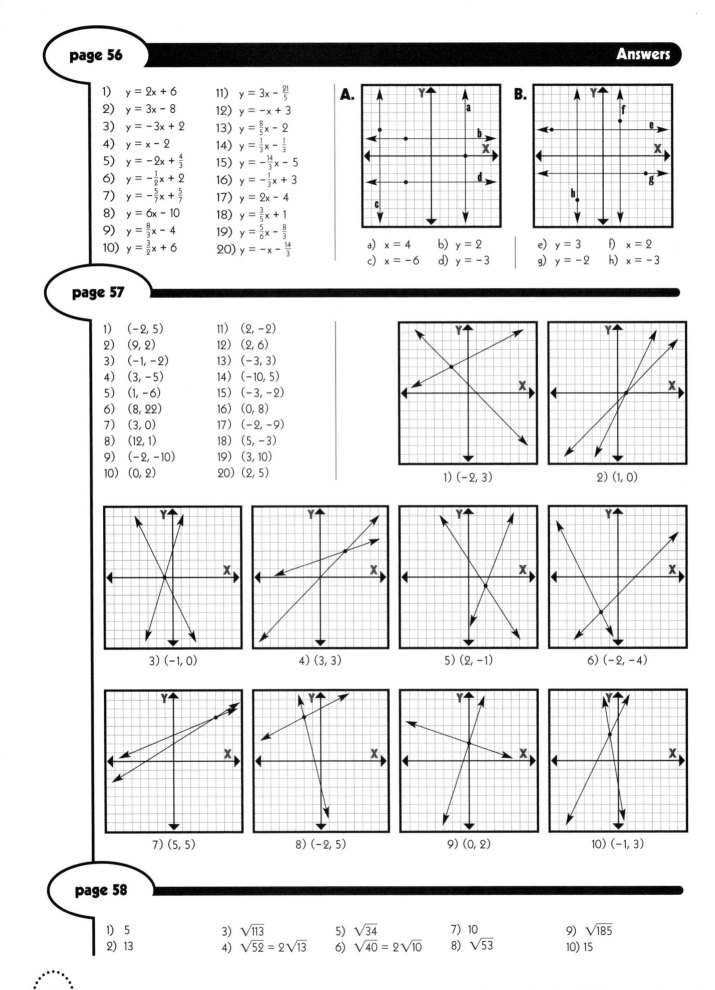

1) 5
2) 13
3) $\sqrt{113}$
4) $\sqrt{52} = 2\sqrt{13}$
5) $\sqrt{34}$
6) $\sqrt{40} = 2\sqrt{10}$
7) 10
8) $\sqrt{53}$
9) $\sqrt{185}$
10) 15

1) $n - 4$
2) $n + 8$
3) $n + 18$
4) $n - 18$
5) $n - 60$
6) $3n$
7) $-n - 7$
8) $-6n$
9) $3(3n - 5)$
10) $-4n + 10$

11) $-(2n - 3)$
12) $6n - 9$
13) $-6n - 9$
14) $6(n - 9)$
15) $9(3n - 6)$

1) $n + 8 = 3n$
2) $(n/100) \cdot 20 = 9$
3) $n + (n + 1) = 15$
4) $(n/100) \cdot 40 = 10$
5) $3(n + 2) = 21$
6) $2(n - 6) = -n$
7) $9 = (30/100) \cdot n$
8) $n = 3(2n - 5)$
9) $-(2n + 1) = 5$
10) $n + (n + 1) + (n + 2) = 33$

11) $6n/5 = n + 2$
12) $(n/100) \cdot 80 = 16$
13) $n + (n + 1) + (n + 2) + (n + 3) = 18$
14) $-4n = n + 10$
15) $30/n = n - 1$

1) $3n + 2 = 11$, so $n = 3$
2) $5(2n - 1) = 25$, so $n = 3$
3) $13n = 4(2n + 5)$, so $n = 4$
4) $4(2n + 6) = 2n$, so $n = -4$
5) $2n + 3 = -n + 6$, so $n = 1$
6) $4n + 6 = 3m - 8$, so $n = -14$
7) $4(-n - 8) = 3n + 3$, so $n = -5$
8) $7(4n - 20) = 8n$, so $n = 7$
9) $5(n - 6) = 2(n + 3)$, so $n = 12$
10) $10n - 4 = 14n$, so $n = -1$

1) 12 is 20% of 60.
2) 5 is 10% of 50.
3) 4 is 2% of 200.
4) 14 is 25% of 56.
5) 45 is 125% of 36.
6) 36 is 90% of 40.
7) 76 is 76% of 100.
8) 54 is 200% of 27.
9) 2 is 40% of 5.
10) 24 is 80% of 30.

1) 75 increased by 20% is 90.
2) 60 increased by 30% is 78.
3) 40 increased by 5% is 42.
4) 12 increased by 50% is 18.
5) 2 increased by 50% is 3.
6) 15 increased by 200% is 45.
7) 56 increased by 25% is 70.
8) 300 increased by 45% is 435.
9) 120 increased by 70% is 204.
10) 80 increased by 35% is 108.

1) 4, 5
2) 12, 14
3) 7, 8, 9
4) 8, 10, 12
5) 12, 13, 14, 15
6) 37, 39
7) 10, 12, 14, 16
8) 41, 43, 45
9) 15, 16, 17, 18, 19
10) 13, 15, 17, 19

1) Eli is 6 years old.
2) Zac is 10 years old.
3) Melanie is 13 years old.
4) Paul is 28 years old.
5) Asher is 21 years old.

1) $d = 45$ miles
2) $r = 9$ mph
3) $t = 2$ hours
4) $r = 12$ mph
5) $d = 300$ miles
6) $r = 20$ mph
7) $d = 24$ miles
8) $t = 5$ hours
9) $r = 13$ mph
10) $t = 2.5$ hours

1) Stacy's dad drives 24 mph.
2) The return trip takes 8 hours.
3) It takes Tony 3 hours.
4) The ski lift travels 600 feet per minute.
5) The boulder rolls down at 64 mph.

1) They will be 44 miles apart.
2) It will be 2 hours until they meet.
3) John's train is travelling at 65 mph.
4) They are 168 miles apart after 6 hours.
5) Jacob walks 6 mph.

Hey! What's this thing?

_____ %

And how do I use it?

In this box, you write the percent of the problems in each section that you got right.

How do you figure that out? Well, until you learn how to work out percent problems on your own, use the handy chart below. You need to know just two things:

(1)   how many problems are in the section, and

(2)   how many of them you answered correctly.

All you to do in order to find your percent correct is multiply the number you got right by the "magic %" number in the chart.

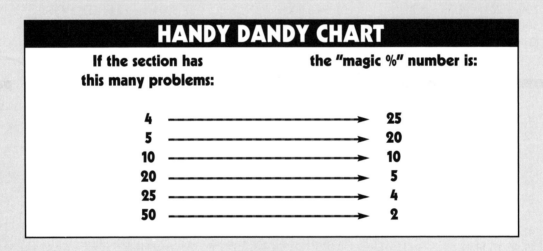

HANDY DANDY CHART

If the section has this many problems:	the "magic %" number is:
4	25
5	20
10	10
20	5
25	4
50	2

Example: Suppose a section you just did has 20 problems, and you got 15 right. Looking at the chart, you see that you need to multiply 15 by 5. This means you got 75% correct. Put that number in the percent box, and that tells you how you did.

But what if your section has a strange number of problems, like 8, 12, 15, 30, or 70? Aha! All you do then is divide the number you got right by the total number of problems, then multiply by 100, and that gives you your percent correct.

Quick example: A section has 70 problems, and you got 59 right. 59 divided 70 equals about 0.84. Multiplying 0.84 by 100, you get 84%. Voilà, there's your percent correct.